WATER THE BAMBOO™

WATER THE BAMBOO™

UNLEASHING
THE POTENTIAL
OF TEAMS AND INDIVIDUALS

GREG BELL

THREE STAR PUBLISHING
PORTLAND, OREGON

Three Star Publishing
1631 NE Broadway #532
Portland, OR 97232
Tel: (503) 963-8817 Fax: (503) 288-3188

Ordering Information

Quantity Sales: Special discounts are available on quantity purchases by corporations, associations, and other organizations. For details, contact Water The Bamboo Center For Leadership toll free at (877) 833-3552.

Individuals Sales: Books are available online at waterthebamboo.com

Printed in the United States of America

Copyediting by Sarah Pagliasotti
Book cover and layout design by Matt Triplett of Sparkplug.com

ISBN-13: 978-1-935313-33-5

First Edition

This book is dedicated to my three girls – whose middle names are Grace, Hope and Joy – and to my lovely wife, Claire, who is the personification of *Water The Bamboo*.

Acknowledgements

This book took a village to grow. It is a culmination of thousands of conversations and observations. While many people participated knowingly, others did so unknowingly; all contributed to making *Water The Bamboo* a reality. My late grandfather, Louis Bell, was a wisdom keeper and an amazing farmer. He encouraged me to think, observe and take risks. I know he would be proud of this book.

To my family who gave me time to put my thoughts on paper, you are my joy and inspiration. Without my wife Claire, there would be no bamboo. Her grace and insight illuminate every page. Hers is the unique ability to envision what exists beyond the reach of the highest giant timber bamboo, while remaining firmly rooted in the rich soil of life. She is something to behold.

Thank you to the readers of this manuscript for your time, energy and smarts. Your input enhanced the quality and content of *Water The Bamboo*; your constructive feedback inspired me and your kind words gave me needed encouragement during stormy times. I am forever indebted to all of you. Linda Collier, Todd Lofgren, Bob Rubery, Shelly Sweeney and Julie Zehetbauer, you all have been infinitely valuable to me in this process. Special thanks to Matt Triplett for the book cover design, book layout, website design, and witty insights.

Special thanks to family and friends whose friendship and encouragement have been extremely helpful:

To Dick Slawson for his love and research, and Lyn Morrison for her gourmet meals, infectious laugh and big hugs. To my father, John Bell, who taught me the value of hard work and stability. To my sister Karen Wilson for her confidence and long phone calls. To Harold and Hedwich "Mom" Jacobs for their warmth and kind spirits. To the late Bob Slawson, a gracious Saint. A special thanks to the late Bryan Johnston, who taught me the importance of values in life and work. Finally, to the late Annett Hunt, my first assistant, who so firmly believed in my work.

Thanks to:

Erica Potechin, Traci Smolen, Terry Taylor, Maggie, Landon Crowell, Isaac Dixon, Enrique Washington, Demian & Bill Lucas, John Lenssen, Judy Clark, Clark Worth, Brian Thomas Wright, Marilyn Cox and her late mother Hazel Engel (both true optimists), David Bartz, Chris Nystrom, Catherine Verhagen, Mark Girard, Chris McKernan, Mark Few, Aaron Thomas, Eric Heinle, Leon P. Rice, Dan Monson, Al Hahn, Julie Harrelson, Patty Farrell, Bob Watkins, Libby Watkins, Sharon VanSickle Robbins, Leo MacLeod, Carrie Hawks, Gail Black, Jonathan Berg, Ron Knight, John Deller, Deborah Dimoff, Jon Eldridge, Bill Ye, Renè Lèger, Richard Fenton, Andrea Waltz, Kevin Carroll, Gary Burke, Joyce Howard, Elaine Sanchez, the late Ralph Bergstrom, Sandra Gray, Peggy Nagae, Betsy Coddington, Chris Daggett, Dan Lucich, David Bond, Jonathan Scherch, Stacy Garret, Tom Vandel, Kal Romine, Jeff Schultz, John Wanberg, Mr. McGill, Chet Nakada, Curtis Wilson, Roland Hoskins, Art & Nancy Hendricks, the late Jim Valvano, and many, many more.

Special thanks to Michelle Jensen Ph.D. for your eagle eye proofreading — your suggestions and thoughts were extremely helpful.

To all of my clients and seminar attendees, over the years you have taken me to some amazing places. I offer you heartfelt thanks. I could not have imagined that so many of you would give me the opportunity to "drop into" your precious lives to do the work that makes my heart sing. I am truly privileged to have spent the past 20 years working with such remarkable leaders and their organizations. Our work together became the springboard for much of what is written in these pages.

Also, thanks to all the writers and speakers who have helped shape my thoughts. I am confident that we have produced a reality-tested book that can help people and their respective teams.

And finally, I am deeply indebted to Sarah Pagliasotti, my extraordinary editor, for her faith, graceful intelligence and guidance. Sarah's ability to keep this project on track and her willingness to be flexible yet strong — like the illustrious bamboo — has been immeasurably precious to this project.

contents

Foreword

It doesn't surprise me a bit that Greg Bell has written a great book designed to help individuals and teams reach their full potential. I would have expected no less. From the time I first met him over 25 years ago, Greg has always been a passionate spokesman for inspiration and achievement. Greg and I were roommates at the University of Oregon, where Greg played on the basketball team and was frequently named "Inspirational Player of the Year".

The seeds of growth Greg has nurtured throughout his career are found within these pages. They are simple, proven effective, and can work for anyone, anywhere. I know this to be true, because I have used many of the same concepts over the years in my role as head basketball coach at Gonzaga University. I am sure Greg used the *Water The Bamboo* approach in developing the Coaches vs. Cancer fundraiser for the American Cancer Society, a program that has raised over $40 million dollars, which Greg was instrumental in getting off the ground. We at Gonzaga proudly participate in helping raise funds for this worthwhile cause and it is even more special because of Greg's early involvement.

Greg argues that I am not a basketball coach but more of a farmer. He's right. When young men enter our basketball program, I believe it is my coaching staffs' responsibility to help them grow and reach their highest potential in every aspect of their lives. Our staff works hard at it, and so do our players. This system has paid off, as many of our players and fans will agree. This success is evidenced with Gonzaga's continued rise over the past decade into the national ranks of college basketball, as well as the success of our players off the basketball court in terms of leadership.

Water The Bamboo is full of timeless messages about growth and achievement. Many of Greg's principles and exercises are variations of what we do with our coaching staff and teams every year. Whether you are a CEO, manager, educator, HR director or ground-level employee, the strategies outlined in this book can help you achieve extraordinary things. They can inspire you and give you a guide to follow. They can also help you get your team to work together as you strive for a common goal. There may be upsets and setbacks along the way, but if you maintain your values, vision and commitment to the plan, you can achieve amazing results.

In basketball, as well as in business or any other endeavor, to succeed you must first truly believe you can do it. All teammates must have faith in themselves and in each other. Whether it's beating a national basketball power on their home floor, or completing a challenging project at work -- if you can envision it, plan for it, and pursue it with dedication and passion, you can come out a winner.

It's my experience that the better your strategy and determination, the more confident you become. That's when the conditions for bamboo-like growth emerge. Our basketball program at Gonzaga is living proof of that. Every member of our team believes we can win, no matter whom we play or where we play. We are not Cinderella hoping for a magical night. We may have been at one time, but no longer. We trust in our system, our individual character and our team effort.

In this book, Greg says you must "practice deliberately." Most people practice the same motions, same steps and same process over and over again, hoping that repetition will produce successful results. But to really improve, you must push yourself beyond what you already know.

Instead of just practicing shots by yourself, for instance, practice them with someone guarding you, with a hand in your face. Practice moves, dribbles and passes that you don't normally try in games, to develop new skills. It's the same in business. This is just one of many insights Greg delivers in his book. There are many others you can put to valuable use.

Go ahead, help yourself. Regardless of what your personal or professional "bamboo" is, this thoughtful book can help you and your team achieve tremendous growth. I'm sure you will benefit from applying the strategies in the following pages. I wish you great success.

Mark Few
Gonzaga University Head Basketball Coach
Winner of the John Wooden Coaching Achievement Award

Welcome to *Water The Bamboo*

What Is the Concept Behind this Book?

Water *The Bamboo* is a metaphor for success. It's a concept based on a type of bamboo that grows like no other plant in the world. Giant timber bamboo can grow 90 feet in 60 days — that's a foot and a half a day! Some claim that you can hear it grow. Wouldn't you like to have that kind of growth in your personal and business life? However, what's even more amazing about giant timber bamboo is that once it's planted, it takes at least three years to break through the ground. Timber bamboo farmers water the seed and tend to it faithfully, even though there's no visible evidence of growth for years.

After more than a decade of working with and studying successful people, teams and organizations, I realized that every person, every team, every family, every organization and every social cause could benefit from understanding the principles giant timber bamboo teaches us about amazing growth and success. What are you working on — or dreaming about — right now, that you won't see results from for years?

The other fascinating fact about this bamboo — which is useful for our analogy — is that you can plant other crops above the bamboo for those three years that it's working its way to the surface. So, you can be working on your bamboo, but also planting corn, beans and any other crop that will help sustain you in the meantime. When you're watering those crops, you're also watering your bamboo.

Water The Bamboo will help you in a number of ways, whether you are a CEO, CFO, vice president, manager, supervisor, HR director, employee, salesperson, educator or a person seeking personal growth. This book will demystify the notion of "overnight success" and provide steps and strategies to help you achieve real growth. I am confident that the ideas and strategies presented in this book will work for you because they've worked and continue to work for thousands of my clients.

Why is this Concept So Important?

Water The Bamboo is the best way to deal with a society plagued with the desire for instant gratification. Based on personal conviction, research, and business experience, *Water The Bamboo* will show you what it really takes to be successful. In this book, you'll learn strategies and walk through the steps to accomplishing amazing growth. This book:

- presents a framework for success

- offers exercises that will tease out your challenges and opportunities

- introduces strategies and mindsets aimed at achievement

- suggests solutions for your own circumstances and personal fulfillment

Full of how-to information and exercises, *Water The Bamboo* will guide you to create your own, personal plan for growth.

Getting the Most Out of This Book

This book is not a cookie-cutter or "quick fix" solution to success; rather it provides a foundation for accessing the answers already within you, your team or your organization. This book is meant to be a guide for your success. *Water The Bamboo* will provide you with practical exercises designed to encourage thought and insight. *Use a separate notebook or journal* as you read along to record your thoughts and responses to the exercises. Anytime the book says "list" or "write," use your journal so your thoughts and responses are all in one central place. This book is user friendly and easy to read. I encourage you to read and re-read it. If you're part of a team, it is helpful for all team members to read it at the same time (like a book club) so that you can discuss the concepts and go through the exercises together. Watering the bamboo in unison can create momentum and focus to ensure new growth in any team or group.

The success of many of my clients continues to validate my theory that the solutions they discover themselves are the ones that work best. The analogies, illustrations and examples in this book are intended to be used as ways to think about the concept. Think in terms of what's important to you and your team as you read, reflect on, and apply each concept. Each chapter is also sprinkled with Bamboo Rules to highlight key points. Below is the first:

Bamboo Rule: The strategies and exercises in this book don't work unless you do.

Let's get real – just like anything in life, you will get out of this book what you put into it. Your success will depend on how you apply yourself, period. You must be involved in the process to reach the growth potential of giant timber bamboo. With this commitment, you will notice greater benefits from your personal development efforts and will discover increased focus, clarity and motivation and greater self-discipline. Read this book as if your future depended on it. It does!

Dreams are great. Making them a reality is better. No matter what your bamboo is, or how seemingly impossible, this book has been designed with one purpose in mind – to guide you into turning your dreams into reality. Today is someday! Let's start watering.

Water The Bamboo Assessment

This tool is designed to give you a quick look at your current situation and rate your areas of strength and weakness – which will give you an idea of the areas you need to focus on. Answering honestly and accurately will help you achieve new levels of growth and set you on the fast track to your dreams. *Remember, this information is just for you!* (Replace "I" with "we" if completing this as a team.)

SKILL	YES	NO	SOME-TIMES
1. I know what my values are and I follow them.			
2. I can picture my vision in my mind.			
3. I have a written action plan on how I am going to achieve my goals.			
4. I have a strategy for building and maintaining my relationships.			
5. I have a strong support network to assist me with my vision.			
6. I believe that I can accomplish my vision.			
7. I focus on my goals and avoid distractions.			
8. My self-talk is positive and helpful.			
9. I have the courage to do what is necessary to achieve my vision.			
10. I regularly show appreciation for myself and others.			
11. I am light-hearted and able to laugh frequently.			
12. I have an optimistic approach.			
13. I have a process for learning new things.			
14. I practice my most critical skills.			
15. I create an environment that is conducive to creativity.			

16. I am comfortable taking the necessary risks to achieve my vision.			
17. I stay committed to my vision despite setbacks.			
18. I have a strategy for effective decision making.			
19. I have the patience to allow something to develop or grow without looking for results too soon.			
20. I deal effectively with change.			
21. I have a balanced life that reflects my values.			
TOTALS			

Scoring:

Give yourself one point for every time you answered "yes," a half point for every time you answered "sometimes" and zero for every time you answered "no."

17 – 21 points. Excellent! You have a good grasp of the principles contained in *Water The Bamboo*. Use this book to help take you to the next level.

12 – 16 points. The *Water The Bamboo* concepts aren't totally new to you, but there are some areas that could use some attention.

Under 12 points. You probably understand some of the *Water The Bamboo* concepts, but will benefit greatly by following the process herein.

If you scored well on the assessment, way to go. But don't relax yet. Individuals and organizations who have had success in the past will still find great value from following the strategies in *Water The Bamboo*. And if you didn't score well, you're taking an important step by reading this book.

PLAN YOUR CROP

one

Dig Deeper – Unearth Your Values

"Things which matter most must never be at the mercy of things which matter least." ~ Goethe

Dissatisfaction, frustration and stress are often caused by people and teams engaging in behavior and activities not aligned with their deeply held values. Success requires that you develop a deep and profound understanding of your own personal values; let them guide you on your journey to success. Success is not defined by financial or material gain, but instead by *daily and long-term living that supports who you are now and who you aspire to be.*

It's a common trap to work long hours striving to achieve a good standard of living. Unfortunately, in the process many people neglect important relationships, personal development and happiness. People and organizations often get pulled in many directions, struggling to keep up with the pace of life, competitors, and the constant flow of tasks and information that must be processed each day. Too many people spend too little time on those things that are truly important. At the end of the day they are exhausted and wonder why they don't feel satisfied. At the end of their lives, they regret not focusing on what mattered most.

Success does not come about by simply engaging in activity; *success is about engaging in activity that matters most to you.* Your task is to find worthy pursuits that have true meaning for you. The fact is, you have limited time and energy in your lifetime, and if you want to keep your spirit nourished and your life in harmony, you have to spend your resources on things that truly matter to you. This doesn't happen accidentally, while you're ticking things off on your to-do list. Achieving success takes conscious effort and clarity about yourself and what you want.

Start by understanding what your deeply held values are, and then by consciously living in harmony with those values on a daily basis. It may sound challenging, but it can make your life easier: you clarify what's important so you schedule time for those things; you avoid the distractions, flirts and external demands of life so you can reserve your precious resources for your highest priorities; you make better decisions because you've run those decisions through your "values filter" to act with clarity and integrity to yourself; and you "walk your talk" so that you are living authentically. You also have more energy at the end of each day because you're honing in on what's most valuable to you, thereby eliminating efforts toward things that are unimportant. It's amazing how much time we all spend on the unimportant – take a look at that for yourself once you clarify your own values.

> **Bamboo Rule: Identifying and talking about your values is the easy part; living up to those values is where the work begins.**

Schedule some time alone to think about what you care about. Consider your various roles and the people in your life. What would you like to contribute? What kind of partner do you want to be? What kind of manager, employee, friend, colleague, parent, child, or sibling do you want to be? Put your values at the center of your life so that your achievements reflect your values.

> ### *Bamboo Rule: Reaching goals while sacrificing your values is not achievement at all.*

Your values should be intrinsically uplifting and motivating. Values reside in your core and call you to a higher place. They are deeply held beliefs that motivate and guide your actions. Values define what you believe in and how you behave. One way to think about values is that everyone's are different. Just like fingerprints, we all have a unique combination of values that show up in everything we do. What gives you the energy to get out of bed in the morning? What motivated you initially to follow the path that you are on? What makes you happy?

> ### *Bamboo Rule: Avoid the temptation to make choices for expediency that are not guided by values.*

Water The Bamboo: Uncover Your Core Values

Read the values on page 13 carefully and select the five that are *most* important to you. (The values listed are just suggestions; if you have other values, use those instead.) Resist the temptation to select more than five – having too many values means you haven't decided what's most important.

1. Don't confuse values and goals – a goal is something you intend to accomplish, whereas a value is an internal belief. The advantage of starting with understanding your values is that you avoid setting a goal that is potentially in conflict with your values.

2. Be sure to choose values you truly care about, not ones you feel you "ought" to choose. What values would create the ideal life for you?

3. Your values can shift. Do you have the same values as you had when you were a teenager? Probably not.

4. After you have selected your five values, ask yourself, "What does each value mean to me?" and, "Why did I choose these?"

5. Next to each of your five core values, list ways you are currently living out that value. Do you notice any gaps between the values you selected and the way you spend your time and energy?

6. Create small goals associated with each value to begin expressing and living your values in your everyday life. Pick something you can do right away that doesn't take a lot of time, energy or money. The sooner you take some action, the more likely you are to follow through.

7. Bring your values to life by choosing one of your five values each week to focus on and highlight or "live" even more.

Bamboo Rule: Walk the talk – work to close any gaps between your espoused values and your behaviors.

Review the list below carefully and circle the five values that are most important to you:

Acceptance	Curiosity	Harmony	Persistence
Accomplishment	Dedication	Health	Pleasure
Accountability	Dependability	Honesty	Religion
Accuracy	Dignity	Honor	Respect
Achievement	Diversity	Hope	Responsibility
Adventure	Empathy	Humor	Security
Ambition	Fairness	Innovativeness	Serenity
Appreciation	Family	Integrity	Service
Beauty	Flexibility	Intelligence	Simplicity
Change	Forgiveness	Joy	Solitude
Collaboration	Friendliness	Kindness	Spirituality
Community	Friendship	Knowledge	Stability
Compassion	Fun	Learning	Strength
Competency	Generosity	Love	Success
Cooperation	Grace	Loyalty	Sustainability
Courage	Happiness	Optimism	Teamwork
Creativity	Hard Work	Peace	Wisdom

Common Team Values Increase Performance

The teams I have worked with who spend time developing their values and working in alignment with them are more focused, energized and happier because they are clear about what's important. They often report dramatic increases in team performance and an improved work environment.

> **Bamboo Example:** *In a survey* of 365 senior executives (one-third of whom were CEOs or board members), the most significant finding was that a large number of companies are making their values explicit. "I see the value of values every day," says Thomas Swartele of France's Bongrain, one of the world's largest cheese companies, doing business in 100 countries. "The communication, the innovation, the adaptability, the coherence: those are the value of values. Because you are approaching markets, problems, and business opportunities from a shared basic belief system, a values-based business approach becomes extremely efficient and powerful."*
>
> **Survey conducted by Booz Allen Hamilton and the Aspen Institute, 2004.*

The values that your organization lives – not the ones that are simply espoused – will shape the organizational culture and drive performance. Posting values in the lobby or break room is not enough. If your organization claims to value work-life balance, for example, but in reality everyone is consistently expected to sacrifice personal time after hours in order to get work done, there's a problem. Such disconnects create cynicism and resentment among your team. It cannot be overstated that values in the workplace are no good – perhaps even counterproductive – if they aren't embodied at all levels of the team or organization. That's why each team member should have a hand in developing his or her group's values. Everyone on your team must be willing to take ownership of the values you establish. Once values are established and agreed upon, it is critical that all team members' actions reflect the group's core values. By explicitly demonstrating and discussing values-directed behavior, team leaders model team values. Allowing a team member to get away with behavior in violation of team values is a no-no. Team leaders must demonstrate team values at all times. It also helps to check in with team members periodically once values are agreed upon, to see how everyone believes the team is living up to them.

Ideas to Keep Team Values Alive

Values are a lot like wedding vows; they must be renewed and revisited to remind the team of why they engaged in the relationship in the first place.

- Refer back to your core values frequently and when you have to make any major decision.

- Discuss values at team meetings or any appropriate opportunity.

- Form a "values committee" charged with making the team's values a reality. For instance, once the team has selected its top five values, the values committee can create draft value guidelines (see sample on page 17) for team approval. As time passes, team members come and go and new team members join, value guidelines serve as a reminder for existing team members and as an orientation for new team members.

- These guidelines work well for reflecting on values as an individual or a family, too.

Water The Bamboo: Creating Team Values

1. As a team and in the context of your work, review the list of values on page 13.

2. Together, discuss the values and pare the list down to five. The value with the most votes may not always be the best choice. Some values are similar to others and both may receive high votes, but after a discussion the team may want to diversify the selection or adopt a value that didn't receive the highest vote initially.

3. Be sure that all team members have an opportunity to participate in the discussion. Arriving as close to consensus as possible will afford the team the most buy-in.

4. Give team members time to reflect on the meaning of the values and how they will apply them on a daily basis.

Personal Values and Team Values

Once you have identified your five core values and your team's five core values, you should have a total of ten values (unless some overlap). Embracing both your personal values and your team's values is key to your success. Your work should be in alignment with your core values, and you should not have difficulty working in alignment with your team's core values. People perform better in jobs and careers when they feel good about the work they're doing, and when their work complements who they are as individuals.

Sample Value Guidelines

Core Value: RESPECT

We **respect** ourselves, our team members, our clients, our vendors, and our communities.

We treat all people with respect, consideration, and fairness. We respect our team members and clients. We encourage and foster a respectful attitude in all areas of life.

Objectives	▪ Respect is reflected in daily behavior and interactions.
	▪ We respect and acknowledge our personal excellence.
Applications	▪ We extend appreciation to those who show respect and who take action against disrespectful behavior.
	▪ We are patient and listen to our team members and clients, and approach each other with an open mind.
	▪ We take care to create a workplace environment that is respectful, safe, and comfortable.
Conversation Starters	▪ How do you define respect?
	▪ What one thing could our team do to better embody the value of respect?
	▪ How do you show respect to your team members? To our clients? To the communities we serve?
	▪ Can you describe a particularly good example of respect in our workplace?

Create a Vivid Vision

"The indispensable first step to getting the things you want out of this life is this: decide what you want." ~ Ben Stein, actor

There is no reason to water weeds. Focus your efforts on your main objective: lush, healthy bamboo. Success requires you to create a picture of what you want – what kind of bamboo, how much, or even the notion to raise bamboo at all. After all, if you don't know what you are working towards, how will you know whether you are making progress? Simply put, you need a compelling vision of what you want.

"Vision without action is a daydream. Action without vision is a nightmare." ~ Japanese proverb

In many organizations and teams, vision is either missing or hazy. Often, teams focus on implementing ideas or taking action before they have dedicated the time to establish a vision and communicate that vision to all team members. People do it, too – how often have you found yourself busy beyond belief, but not getting any closer to what you really want? What's the point of climbing to the top of the ladder of success if you realize, in the end, that you're on the wrong wall?

Don't Skip This Step!

There are no excuses for not creating your vision. Studies show that great organizations and great achievers have a compelling vision and they follow that vision passionately. People and groups often complain that they don't have time to create their visions. You don't have time *not* to create one, because without a vision you are guaranteed to waste time getting sidetracked by non-essentials. You would find it absurd to go to the airport and ask for a ticket without telling the ticket agent where you want to go!

Ask yourself: "What do I want to create? Is my idea or activity connected to my values? What would make me proud to be part of?" Take time to visualize compelling and exciting possibilities for your team and for yourself, both personally and professionally.

Avoid the Negative Feedback Loop

Often, people react negatively to conversations about vision. They say things like:

- "Talking about vision is a waste of time; we need action"

- "We did that a few years ago (and haven't looked at it since)"

- "This vision is unrealistic"

- "Talk is cheap – we want results"

- "What will others say about my dreams if I express them openly?"

Most people are not used to talking about what they really want. People report feeling childish and vulnerable when expressing their dreams and hopes. We habitually share cynicisms and frustrations without hesitation, but it's somehow harder to share our hopes and dreams or encourage that in others. Even when good things happen, people say things like "We got a lucky break." Those who water their bamboo to phenomenal growth start the process by envisioning how it will look at the end. They express their deepest desires and dynamic visions with the same energy that ordinary people give to cynicism and negativity.

A compelling vision of what success looks like stimulates passion, focus and enthusiasm for its attainment. Inventors, athletes, business leaders and top students use vision and visualization to achieve superior performance. Now is the time to rise to your full potential – no holding back. Why are you on the planet? What is your dream? What do you want to contribute?

Bamboo Rule: You must retreat to advance.

Water The Bamboo: Envisioning Your Bamboo

Bamboo farmers don't start in haste; they plan before they plant. So should you. Take some uninterrupted time alone or with your team. Start by relaxing and being quiet so that the most powerful computer in the world – your brain – can get a much-needed "time out" from the usual, break-neck pace of life. Let your mind wander for a while; just daydream. Great visions are created in the mind and heart. Let life's chatter and demands die down so that your brain can "hear" your heart. Relax and review your values. Close your eyes; take some deep breaths. Write down answers to the following questions: What do you want to accomplish in life and in your work? What are you striving for? What is so crucial to your success that you are willing to work on it, possibly for years, without seeing results? Get creative: ask yourself, "If I could do anything, be anything, create anything, what would it be?" Or ask, "If we had unlimited resources what would we want to achieve or create?" Keep brainstorming; there will be plenty of time for refining your list later. This is no time to be realistic. Go crazy!

> *"Dream what you want to dream; go where you want to go; be what you want to be, because you have only one life and one chance to do all the things you want to do." ~ Anonymous*

For a group brainstorm, you might first want to set ground rules, such as no interrupting or criticizing someone's idea. You can either have folks write down their own ideas first and create a collective list, or do the brainstorming out loud as a group.

Other questions to ask:

- Who do I/we want to be?

- What do I/we want to have?

- What do I/we want to do?

- How do I/we want to be known?

Water The Bamboo: Create Your Professional Vision

- Take a moment to remember your first days at your current work situation. Remember how excited you were. What drove or inspired you?

- Then read through the following sentences and answer as if your work life were exactly as you would like it to be. Let this be an optimistic reflection of what you envision for your *ideal work life* three years from now. Get as specific as you want; don't just limit yourself to the following questions.

- My career focus is in the areas of...

- My work environment is...

- My work philosophy is...

- My daily work life consists of…

- I feel successful at work when…

Water The Bamboo: Create a Vision Statement

After you have completed all these pieces of your professional vision, write a summary paragraph that encapsulates all your intentions and desires. This is your vision statement. Write a rough draft and then polish it in the weeks to come. In your journal, complete the following sentence:

In my professional life my vision is to…

Water The Bamboo: Create a Vision Board

As you are working on your vision, it should meet the "three Vs": your vision should be *visible* and *vivid* to be *viable*. Once you have created a picture of your bamboo in your mind, make it visible and vivid. Put it down on paper. Or fabric. Or whiteboard – whatever works. It could just be the vision statement you created, or it could be some other representation that works for you. But make it as vivid as you can. Add details and color (literally and figuratively) so that the vision is alive and compelling. You may want to cut out pictures that represent your vision. For example, you could have pictures of your satisfied clients, the cutting-edge work space you envision for yourself, or your family spending time together because you've achieved that elusive work-life balance. Whatever your vision is, make it come alive so that it can energize you and remind you why you're watering your bamboo whenever you look at it. Frame your vision board and keep it in a place where you can see it every day.

Team Vision

If you work in a team, you're obviously going to be balancing multiple visions. You are likely asked to follow the existing vision of the organization and perhaps a vision that your particular team creates, in addition to having your own professional and personal vision. Ideally, those visions are aligned, or at least overlap in some areas.

Once you've created your own professional vision, look for opportunities for your organization's vision and yours to be mutually supportive. Sometimes, pursuing your own vision requires aligning with the vision or dreams of others, whether it's the organization you work for or the clients you serve.

Vision Ownership

It may seem challenging to embrace your organization's vision if you weren't involved in creating it. It can feel like something imposed on you, rather than something you truly believe in. But you're working with your organization for a reason, so naturally there must be some aspects of its vision that you inherently support. Here's an example that illustrates this point:

> *Bamboo Example: At a local hospital, there were three nurses working in different departments. The first is asked, "What are you doing?" and replies, "Checking in this patient." The second is asked, "What are you doing?" The reply is, "Feeding my family." The third is asked, "What are you doing?" and replies, "I'm here to make a difference in the health of our community."*

To embrace your organization's vision:

1. Start by understanding it. If it's not readily available, ask your team or group leader for a copy or have them articulate it.

2. Then ask yourself:

    a. What resonates with me about this vision? What do I like about it?

    b. What can I do on a daily basis that supports making this vision a reality?

3. If you're struggling to answer those questions or to understand how the vision applies to you, discuss it with your coworkers, supervisor or someone else. Your willingness to explore the vision will speak volumes about your desire to help create success.

The work of watering the bamboo starts with a compelling vision that is rooted in your values. But that's only the beginning. You must take the time and effort to put what you want on the agenda. Big dreams aren't realized immediately – but they're not realized at all without a vision today. Hold on to your vision, but be flexible about how you get there. Frequently revisit your vision to see whether it still makes sense. Obstacles and adversity are certain, but with tenacity and flexibility you will achieve what you envision.

No Goals, No Bamboo

"If you aim at nothing, you'll hit it every time." ~ Anonymous

Now that you have established your values and created a compelling vision, you can shift your attention to the day-to-day activities that will make it happen: goals. Goals answer the question, "How do we get there?" While your vision focuses on the big picture and is more strategic, goals are tactical – goals help you achieve your vision.

Goals guide your daily activities; they serve as milestones that help you know you are moving in the right direction. And, they should be flexible: when necessary, goals are adjusted to make course corrections as new resources, information, opportunities and obstacles arise.

To accomplish a great vision you will need laser-like focus. Effort without a plan is never enough. Without goals and purpose, you will simply drift haphazardly. Establishing and pursuing your goals is a way of putting your life in good hands – your own!

Goals will help you:

- improve performance

- strengthen self-confidence

- increase motivation

- sharpen focus

- establish priorities

Creating and Accomplishing Effective Goals

Base Your Goals on Your Values and Vision. If your goals are harmonious with your values and vision, you are more likely to accomplish them. Aligning your goals with your values helps you make choices that will reduce the stress caused by conflicting demands on your time and energy. For example, if your primary goal is to double your income within the next two years, and you have to work 12 hours per day to accomplish that, you could have a problem if one of your top values revolves around your family. To be truly successful in any endeavor, your values, vision and goals all need to align. And, you should be clear about the benefits of reaching those goals in terms of your overall vision of what you want from life. Prioritize your goals by letting them flow from your values and vision.

> *Bamboo Rule: Having too many goals is*
> *the same as having **no goals**.*

Write Your Goals Down and Develop an Action Plan. Writing down your goals is your commitment to achieving your vision. Clearly articulated, written and visible goals are much more powerful than some loosely held thoughts in the back of your mind. Create action plans and due dates to make goals even more powerful and tangible. (See the exercise on page 30 on how to develop an action plan.)

Seek Guidance and Help. A mentor or coach can help you with your action plan by providing motivation and serving as a sounding board.

Review Your Goals Daily. Reading your goals each day prior to setting your daily agenda serves as a reminder for you to stay focused. You are more likely to accomplish the goals you set if you review them regularly as part of your normal planning process.

Bamboo Rule: What gets measured gets done.

Monitor Goals Progress Regularly. Consistently measure your progress against your efforts and plans to assure you are working effectively. If you are a manager or team leader, make sure this is happening for your team.

Re-check Your Goals Against Your Vision. Just tracking your goals is not enough. Every so often, ask yourself questions such as, "Is this still the right priority for my vision? Should I adjust my goals based on new information?"

Celebrate As You Go. Celebrate accomplishments large and small. Honor yourself for what you have achieved, and if you are on a team, honor your team members' successes. Then move on to the next milestone.

Bamboo Rule: Every day, take some action towards your goals.

What To Do with Barriers to Your Goals

Are there specific obstacles you are experiencing that are interfering with your ability to accomplish your goals? If so, identify the obstacle and brainstorm potential root causes. This will help you decide how to address the challenge.

If you are still not making progress on a particular goal, *stop* and honestly analyze why you are not moving forward. Review your vision board and recommit to your vision.

Ask yourself:

- Are there other approaches?

- Who can I ask who may be a good resource?

- What kind of help can I get from co-workers, friends or family?

> *Bamboo Rule: Obstacles are what you see*
> *when you take your eyes off your goal.*

Water The Bamboo: Create Your Goals and Action Plan

Read your vision statement. Brainstorm all of the things you can do that will get you closer to your vision. It may help to consider the following questions:

- What actions will help me make the most significant progress toward my vision?

- What is the thing that I least want to do that is necessary for me to achieve my vision?

- Can large projects be broken into small, manageable tasks?

Once you have a comprehensive list of ideas, evaluate all of these goals and tasks by importance – which are the most important to you achieving your vision? Those should be your priority – a smaller subset on which you spend most of your time and energy. And each goal may comprise multiple tasks. Schedule these tasks, and the goals you're working toward, on your calendar: what you will do each day and what milestones you will reach. Once you've done this, you'll see that any vision – no matter how seemingly unreachable – can be accomplished with a system of goals, tasks and an action plan. Then, resolve to water your bamboo – working on your most important goals – each day.

Bamboo Rule: Seek progress, not perfection.

DON'T FARM ALONE

four

Tend Your Relationships

"Light is the task when many share the toil." ~ Homer

Let's face it, this is the relationship age! The information age is over – there is too much of it, everyone has access to it, and much of it is not useful. Your success depends on the quality of your relationships. Get on the relationship-age bus or be run over by it. The old saying, "It's who you know, not what you know" is more true now than ever. Individuals and teams who understand this will thrive in these changing times.

> *Bamboo Rule: The quality of your bamboo will be determined by the quality of your relationships.*

We celebrate the individual as being "self made" and tend to forget that success takes teamwork and relationships. We know household names and faces like Bill Gates, Oprah, Tiger Woods, Lance Armstrong, and Jay Leno; however, we do not see the thousands of people who support their efforts or help them achieve greatness. Do you think that any of them could be as successful without the help of others?

Bamboo Rule: No person is an island.

Most of us learned what we know about relationships from our parents, television and by trial and error – lots of error. Great relationships are an essential ingredient of healthy, productive, and effective home and work environments. However, after years of experience most people still struggle with them.

Bamboo Rule: Your ability to have effective relationships will do far more for you than any other skill you learn.

Computers and other equipment receive a lot of attention and resources – they can be fixed or even replaced, but damage to a relationship is much more difficult to heal. Breakdowns in relationships cost more in lost time, money, productivity, and efficiency than do technical problems.

How Do You Build Relationships?

Most people only work on strengthening their relationships when there are problems. That's like taking vitamins only *after* you become sick.

Has anyone ever sat you down and said the following: "This is how you build and maintain deep, long lasting, authentic relationships," or at least given you some direction? Probably not. If you're one of the many people on earth who never had a class or received a road map for building effective relationships, here's your chance to learn an easy-to-use, four-stage model that I developed and have used to train thousands of people and organizations to help them build effective professional and personal relationships.

Relationship Map

GregBell Curve®

Build Trust	Cultivate	Take Risks	Empowerment
		SKILLS / COMPETENCIES	
Respect	Empathy	Vulnerability	Accept
Open-ended Questions	Self Disclose Values	Give Effective Feedback	Include
Listening	Seek Input	Support	Value
	Find Common Ground		
		BEHAVIORS	
Attend (show up)	Share Authority	Initiate Contact	Openness
Observe	Problem Solve	Leave Comfort Zone	Confidence
Suspend Judgment	Personalize Opinions		

STAGE I   STAGE II   STAGE III   STAGE IV

The graphic above lays out the four stages people go through to reach an effective and mutually empowering relationship, and outlines the skills and behaviors required at each stage. This model is intended to serve as a guide, but note that relationships are dynamic and are not one-size-fits-all, so you may move back and forth from one stage to another, or get to empowerment sooner with one person than another. In fact, you may think you are at one stage with a person and they think you are at another. The bell curve and shaded area represent the amount of time and energy required at each stage of a relationship. You'll notice in Stage I, Build Trust, the investment of time and energy is less than in Stages II and III, where you have to engage in skills and behaviors like self disclosure, vulnerability and leaving your comfort zone. Since the skills in Stage I put the focus on the other person, not as much effort is required. Notice that less energy is required in Stage IV as well. The presumption is that you have put in the work in the previous stages. For example, you are more likely to be open and confident with an old friend even if you haven't seen them in a while, because you already moved through the other stages. The goal is to get to Stage IV, Empowerment, in all your key relationships, especially those on whom your bamboo is dependent. The key is to water and tend to relationships before you need them.

Bamboo Rule: Don't let promising relationships wilt due to neglect or lack of watering.

Benefits of Watering Your Relationships

By watering and improving your relationships, you will gain resources such as information, energy, work efficiencies, income, ideas, and increased productivity.

In fact, as you move from Stage I to Stage IV, your resources increase steadily while your investment of time and energy decreases.

Resources Increase Over Time

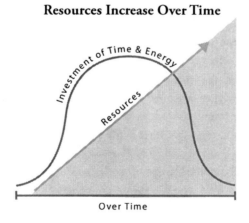

The following is a narrative description of the four stages of communication based on the Relationship Map on the previous page. These are the highlights of each stage, which should help you as you think about relationships and how they impact watering your bamboo.

> **"Organizations are no longer built on force, but on trust." ~ Peter Drucker**

Stage 1: Build trust. Trust is built through actions not just words. The original purpose of most traditional greetings was based on establishing trust. In medieval Europe, kings and knights shook hands to demonstrate that they did not have a concealed weapon. Bowing exposed the most vulnerable area of the body (the top of the head), and the salute represented raising the visor (back in the day of armor) to see the other person and establish friend or foe. In today's world, the skills and competencies of respect, asking open-ended questions, and listening are intended to show the receiver you are interested in building trust with them. Behaviors such as showing up, observing, and suspending judgment reinforce your genuine interest. Asking open-ended questions such as those that start with who, what, where, when and how allow the receiver to tell their story and give you an opportunity to listen to them and allow them to be heard, thereby feeling respected. (Note: it is best to avoid "why" at this stage as it can cause defensiveness when brought up too early in the developing relationship.)

Stage 2: Cultivate. This stage takes more energy and effort than Stage I. Behaviors here include engaging in empathy and self-disclosure with the other person. You are seeking things you have in common. You're also sharing authority, seeking input and collaborating to problem-solve. Personalize your opinions rather than making absolute statements that assert your authority or expertise. In this process, it's helpful to use "I" statements such as "I think," "I feel," and "I want."

Stage 3: Take risk. Taking risk is important in building lasting relationships. Risk-taking requires you to be vulnerable and face possible rejection and embarrassment. Like learning to juggle, you must be willing to miss while you are acquiring the skill. Challenge yourself to reach out to someone whom you normally wouldn't talk to or to initiate an invitation to someone with whom you've recently met.

Stage 4: Empowerment. This is where we all want our relationships to be. Here, we're open and confident in our relationships. That means accepting, including and valuing people. Here we're enjoying the benefits of our previous relationship efforts. Because of deep trust and positive past experiences, we can depend on one another and make requests we wouldn't if we were still in Stage I.

Valuing Differences

In any group, and in most relationships, people bring different skills. You may have chosen your spouse or partner because their strengths balanced out your weaknesses, and vice versa. Work groups are composed of people with a variety of skills, experience and perspectives – making the group stronger than if everyone were like-minded and similarly talented. Your two hands are equal and opposite. Your left hand may be holding this book while your right hand turns the pages. Notice that one hand isn't jealous of the other. If one hand gets tired, the other can compensate. It's this kind of synergy between people that makes for empowering relationships, effective work groups, and success.

Bamboo Rule: If two people have exactly the same thoughts, one person is unnecessary.

Stop, Look and Listen!

Stop. Our dealings with people are often quick transactions – we need something from someone so we interact with them. But at times we do so too quickly and with too much focus on the result we want from the interaction. We risk treating people as if they were vending machines or drive-through restaurants instead of showing them respect and patience. Slow down and take the time to develop quality relationships. They will help you get the results you are after.

Look. Make it a practice to observe body language. How do people respond to you and others? Observing behavior will inform beyond mere words. Be a student of the non-verbal aspects of your interactions.

Listen. Most conversations are like tennis matches: you talk, then the other person responds, with no space for real listening. We are often distracted by what we are going to say next while the other person is speaking. It's frustrating for the person talking, and the "listener" only hears a fraction of what was said. As a result, communication breaks down, deadlines are missed, and expectations aren't met.

Improving your listening skills is one of the best things you can do to improve your relationships. Fortunately, listening is a skill you can improve on by paying attention and practicing. Here's a helpful tip: what word can you make from the letters in the word "listen" that will help you be a better listener? The answer is S-I-L-E-N-T.

Bamboo Rule: The magic of music is the silence between the notes.

Formula for Handling People by General George C. Marshall, US Secretary of State:

1. Listen to the other person's story.
2. Listen to the other person's full story.
3. Listen to the other person's story first.

Vow to become a better listener by using the following tips:

- Practice receiving people's communication without:
  - interrupting them
  - finishing their sentences
  - mentally jumping ahead
  - thinking about yourself or what you'll say next
  - filling in the blanks of what they say with what you already believed anyway

- Keep in mind that you learn less when you are talking than when you are listening.

- Realize that you have the right to convince, persuade and influence others, but they also have these same communication rights. Sometimes it is wiser to be kind than to be right.

- Being a good listener does not mean that you agree with what you are hearing, or subscribe to the values and opinions of the speaker.

- Sometimes it helps the speaker if you simply listen to them before beginning to problem-solve.

- Be aware of your biases and prejudices so that they do not filter out an important part of the speaker's message.

- Know your own hot buttons so that you can avoid responding to emotionally charged words and phrases. Sometimes silence is golden.

- Stay curious and avoid mind reading – particularly around people you know well. Wait until a person has finished speaking before you respond.

- Paraphrase what the speaker said and ask, "Did I understand that right? Would you like to say more?" If there's an adjustment or more information, paraphrase again.

Bamboo Rule: You have two ears and one mouth. Use them accordingly.

If All Else Fails...

Remember these two rules as you're engaging with others:

- Golden Rule: "Do unto others as **you** would have them do unto you."

- Platinum Rule: "Do unto others as **they** would have you do unto them." ~ Dr. Tony Alessandra, author

Water The Bamboo: Watering Your Relationships

1. You are not alone. Make a list of the people who have made a positive impact on your life and success so far – parents, teachers, friends, mentors, coaches, authors, colleagues, managers, spiritual leaders, neighbors, etc.

2. Make a list of the key relationships that may help you successfully grow and harvest your bamboo. Is there a person you value and want to get to know better?

3. Where are you with each of those relationships on the Relationship Map (i.e., what stage)?

4. What activities can you engage in to help move those relationships to the next stage? What activities can you do to maintain your relationships?

Water The Bamboo: Improve Your Listening

In your journal, list three things you can do to become a better listener.

Create or Join a Bamboo Circle

"None of us is as smart as all of us." ~ Ken Blanchard

A Bamboo Circle is a group of people who get together to help each other on the journey to success. Wouldn't it be great to be part of a group whose main purpose was to help each other achieve your respective visions and goals? A Bamboo Circle is just that – a group that meets on a regular basis who listens and brainstorms solutions and strategies, and generally supports and helps each other be accountable.

How It Works

In a Bamboo Circle, members meet regularly (typically once a month – teams can use their staff meetings). Each member gets a "turn" at each meeting, so that everyone is supported to continually make and track his or her progress. In the initial meetings, members use their turn to share their visions or their understanding of the team's vision and outline the goals and milestones they've identified toward reaching that vision.

Bamboo Circle members ask questions, offer suggestions and brainstorm helpful tips and ideas to solidify others' goals and plans. In subsequent meetings, all members report their progress on the goals they've committed to working toward. Once a milestone is reached, members commit to a new one to be presented at the next meeting.

The benefits of participating in a Bamboo Circle include:

- the opportunity to perform at a higher level because like-minded people can help you make better decisions while holding you accountable

- the opportunity to confide in a group of trusted advisors with confidence about challenges or barriers to your vision and goals

- getting to know colleagues you respect while helping them grow their bamboo

Things to Think About as You Form Your Bamboo Circle

Like each other first. Don't go into this thinking that good individuals in a room will become a good team. It doesn't usually work that way. Make sure you have a small group of people who are already like-minded and have some connection with one another – but who aren't so similar that you all have the same expertise or backgrounds.

Have the right purpose in mind. The focus of a Bamboo Circle is to help participants independently achieve their visions and goals. It's not about being overly dependent on the group, and it's not a group counseling or complaint session. Ensure that everyone invited to the group is aware of its purpose so that the group doesn't turn into a social occasion.

Participate. The group won't work without everyone's participation. Affirm that everyone is expected to share what their bamboo is, as well as the milestones they need to accomplish towards its growth. Members should be prepared to ask for help and offer suggestions or resources when others express a need.

Keep the numbers low. The number in the group should remain low – five to six members is ideal. More than seven members is usually too many. (Note: for large work teams or departments, create natural sub-teams if necessary.) A smaller group allows each participant to get the support and appropriate focus they need. A strong group has enough people to contribute a variety of energies and ideas, but not so many that it's difficult to tend to each member's needs.

As a rule, have rules in place. Set ground rules regarding attendance, lateness, agenda, format, logistics, frequency of meetings, confidentiality, facilitation, membership, and various other aspects of conducting a successful meeting. (See sample ground rules on the next page.)

Be goal-oriented. At the end of every meeting, recap the goals each member has committed to. These should be revisited at the beginning of the next meeting. This will ensure that the group holds each other accountable to commitments.

Stay focused. Time is your most valuable resource – don't waste yours! It's easy to have the meeting cluttered with social niceties; don't let this derail your circle. Keep the light social stuff to five minutes before or after the meeting.

Be on the same page. Ideally members have already read *Water The Bamboo* and have completed the exercises contained therein, especially the design of their vision boards.

Be committed to the meeting. With few exceptions, the meeting should be as important as any appointment or even a paid engagement.

Have a convener. Select someone in the group to keep everyone on task. There are always members of a group who don't keep their promises, show up late, miss meetings and are downright unreliable. The convener deals with this and may bring it to the group's attention. The role of the convener can rotate every 3-6 months.

Have fun. It may not be karaoke or bowling, but you should enjoy spending time with your Bamboo Circle. If you're lucky, it'll turn into playtime.

Know when to fold them. If the Bamboo Circle meetings don't seem to click after three or four meetings, bring the discussion up in the meeting. Discuss what's not working and see if it can be resolved. If it can't, cut it loose and start anew.

Sample Ground Rules

1. **Start meetings on time.** Don't backtrack to fill in a member who is late. If someone knows they will be late, they should inform the group or group convener. Consider establishing a cut-off point: if you're going to be more than 15 minutes late, skip the meeting out of respect to the others.

2. **End meetings on time.** This shows respect for everyone's time and underscores the importance of starting on time and staying on track.

3. **Notice.** Notify the convener if you will miss a meeting.

4. **Time limits.** Each group member will have 10 minutes at each meeting. A timekeeper should be assigned to keep the meeting on track. If someone needs more time at a particular meeting it is possible to ask for another person's time.

5. **Confidentiality.** Everyone should agree to keep disclosures and
    details from each meeting confidential. If you choose to share your
    own experiences in the group you can; however, you are not allowed
    to share details about another member's experience.

6. **Order of participation.** Establish how you will proceed through
    the group at each meeting. For example, rotate alphabetically at one
    meeting and in reverse order at the next.

7. **Respect.** Only one person talks at a time, and everyone gives that
    person his or her full attention – absolutely no interrupting. Take
    notes to retain comments and questions.

8. **Leaving the group.** If a group member wants to quit the Bamboo
    Circle they will let the group know ahead of time, preferably with an
    explanation or feedback that can help the circle improve.

9. **Terminating membership.** If the group feels that a member
    consistently violates ground rules or is not participating, the group
    can decide to terminate the person's membership.

10. **Adding members.** Before adding any new members, the group must
    unanimously agree to do so. Provide a thorough orientation for the
    new member that may include one-on-one conversations with each
    member designed to build trust and bring the new member up to
    speed.

USE THE BAMBOO FARMER'S TOOLS

Belief

"To succeed, we must first believe that we can." ~ Michael Korda, novelist

What has ever been accomplished that wasn't rooted in the belief that it was possible? Even though setbacks and challenges occurred at some level, belief remained. When you believe, you take actions to make it so. What could you accomplish right now if you believed it were possible from the start?

Belief operates like an "on" and "off" switch: when it's on, it can provide instant energy; when it's turned off, it can just as quickly kill the power of an idea. No matter what you set out to do, your belief or non-belief is a highly pivotal factor in whether you accomplish your goal. When you plant the seed of your vision you must believe it will grow, otherwise you won't put in the energy and effort necessary for success. Take an inventory of your beliefs as they relate to your vision. Are they supporting you or standing in your way?

"One person with a belief is equal to a force of ninety-nine
who have only interests." ~ John Stuart Mill, philosopher

Beliefs allow you to tap into your deepest potential and work almost like magic. For proof, look no further than the "placebo effect" – where people recover from ailments with nothing but sugar pills and a belief they've taken a medicine that will cure them. The placebo effect is similar to Expectancy Theory – one example of which is how students' achievements often match their teachers' expectations of them. What you project or expect, happens.

> ***Bamboo Example:*** *A struggling junior sales associate went to a senior associate and asked for some sales leads. The senior associate gave her a list of ten qualified leads and said that she should call them right away because "They're waiting for your call." The junior associate made successful sales to seven out of the ten leads. Excitedly, she went back to the senior associate for more leads. The senior associate gave her the telephone book and said, "Here you go. This is where I got the first ten!"*

People who have great success are just like you – seemingly ordinary people – but they have developed a powerful and unwavering conviction and expectation that they will achieve their visions. Imagine if Southwest Airlines founder Herb Kelleher had believed all the people who told him he'd never be able to compete with the big airlines. What if Phil Knight, founder of Nike, had become discouraged by critics who told him the athletic shoe had a limited market?

Bamboo Rule: Beliefs command the mind into action or inaction.

A belief is either empowering or limiting. Identify your beliefs associated with growing your bamboo. What beliefs occupy your mind? Notice the difference between the limited and expansive beliefs listed on next page:

Limited Belief	Expansive Belief
• This is the way that we've always done it. • It'll cost too much. • We don't have what it takes to accomplish this.	• Let's give the new way a try; it may create new opportunities. • The value it brings could outweigh the cost. • We can build the right partnerships and alliances to get it done.

The subconscious can't tell what is real or imagined. If there is something that you desire, your subconscious must believe it is possible to attain it. Train your subconscious to support what you want to be true.

Bamboo Rule: Whether you believe you will be successful or you believe you won't – you are right.

It takes no more effort to believe than it does to doubt. While doubt is draining, belief energizes you to do the things that will make the belief a reality. When people or teams believe they will succeed, they bring their best efforts, they persist past obstacles and they consistently find evidence that they're on the right path.

Five Ways to Create a Strong Belief in Yourself:

1. **When belief withers, nurture it with possibilities.** As you're watering your bamboo, you will likely encounter obstacles, naysayers, and self-doubt. While you're working your way past these challenges,

think about all the reasons why *you can* succeed rather than the reasons you can't. One technique is to simply say, "It may not be true today, but I am finding ways to make it happen."

2. **Fake it 'til you make it.** What may seem like forced belief at first will, with practice, become real belief that grows more unwavering day by day, month in and month out, year by year. So keep nurturing it, even if it doesn't come naturally.

3. **Practice with others.** While you're cultivating the habit of belief in yourself and your vision, practice with other people. The next time someone in your department or on your team puts forth a new idea, make it a policy not to discuss why it won't work until you fully explore all the ways you can make it work.

4. **Retrain your brain with affirmations.** Wake up every morning and say to yourself 10 times:

    -   "I believe in myself and my team."

    -   "I believe in my vision."

    -   "I believe I will succeed."

    The more you repeat these thoughts, the more they become a natural part of you on both a subconscious and conscious level.

5. **Seek inspiration from other people's successes.** Read inspiring quotes or stories about people who succeeded against seemingly overwhelming obstacles, or about "regular" people who accomplished something special. These tales will remind you of the power of possibilities. Also look for people in your life and your work whom you admire; pay attention to the beliefs they demonstrate.

Five Ways to Develop Belief about Your Vision

1. Read your vision statement and look at your vision board. Now, imagine your vision as the current reality.

2. Follow the goals you set – do something every day to work towards your vision.

3. Act as if you have already accomplished your vision: dress and behave as the person you want to be. If you want to be a leader, walk, talk and act like a leader today.

4. Get support. A coach, mentor or your Bamboo Circle can help you stay focused and accountable.

5. Have great expectations!

*"It's the repetition of affirmations that leads to belief.
And once that belief becomes a deep conviction, things
begin to happen." ~ Claude M. Bristol, author*

seven

Self-Discipline

"With self-discipline most anything is possible." ~ Theodore Roosevelt

Great achievement and success are largely the consequence of self-discipline. Of course, circumstances and ability play a role as well, but research has shown that your daily actions will have a much greater impact on whether your bamboo grows than talent or luck.

Self-discipline is best defined as the ability to control your conduct by using sound judgment, rather than allowing yourself to be driven by impulse or emotion. Self-discipline operates twofold: on the one hand it is your ability to take the necessary action for success; on the other hand it is your ability to say no to activities that could take you off target. People and organizations who stay focused on their vision and goals and consistently follow their priorities tend to succeed in any endeavor.

Bamboo Example: Speaking to an audience of college graduates, famous investor Warren Buffet said, "Everybody here has the ability to do anything I do and much beyond. Some of you will, and some of you won't. For those of you who won't, it will be because you get in your own way, not because the world does not allow you to."

Bamboo Rule: Get out of your own way.

Disciple Thyself

The word "discipline" comes from the same root as "disciple," a root that means "to teach." Think of self-discipline as a form of teaching yourself – you can remember it as "disciple thyself." Be your own teacher and your own disciple. You have the wisdom and the will to do what you need to do, but as a disciple of yourself you must listen to that wisdom and practice your own teachings.

"Discipling" yourself also means controlling yourself. Is there something you can do in the next day to destroy any hope of your dream coming true? Is there something you can do today to move you closer to your dream? You probably answered yes to both questions. Now ask yourself, whose choice is it? You have ultimate control in your life over the choices you make. What power! A person who is clear about what they want and who has made discipline a habit can succeed at almost anything.

Bamboo Rule: Self-mastery is the prerequisite to success.

Discipline is, at heart, a choice. So if it's a choice, then you can make that choice a habit, because habits are nothing more than choices that are so ingrained they become predetermined. Successful people have a habit of doing what unsuccessful people are not willing to do. You get to choose which habits you're going to create.

> *"Greatness is not a function of circumstance, it's a function of choice and discipline."* ~ *Jim Collins, author*

What if you or your team had the self-discipline to follow through on your intentions? How would your life, your career or your organization be different? You might be saying to yourself "I just don't have self-discipline; I never have." But everyone has *some* self-discipline. You work. You care for a pet, children, or yourself – maybe even all three. It took a certain amount to get this far in this book. Congratulations! Since self-discipline is the lifeblood of success, the challenge is to create more. And you don't have to have self-discipline in every aspect of your life. But for phenomenal bamboo growth, *you have to develop it in those areas that are most important to your happiness and success.*

Seven Practical Ideas for Building Self-Discipline:

1. **Welcome and recognize your own responsibility.** It's up to you to take responsibility for your own self-discipline. Accept where you are right now, without shame or guilt. Today is a new day and a new opportunity to water your bamboo.

2. **Remember you've done it before.** Recall a time or situation where you demonstrated self-discipline, and where it got you. How did you feel?

3. **Expect temptation, but don't be diverted by it.** Pressure to take an easier route or be distracted by another pleasure is inevitable. For example, imagine it's time to practice an important skill or complete an important task and someone invites you for coffee or a movie. A person working to increase their self-discipline says something like, "Coffee sounds nice, but it's not going to take me where I want to go." When approached with a tempting invitation, ask yourself,

"Does this support my vision or one of my core values?" If not, smile and politely decline.

> *"Those who mind don't matter and those*
> *who matter don't mind." ~ Dr. Seuss*

4. **Relax.** Some think self-discipline has to be tense and strenuous. There is nothing further from the truth. In fact, it's usually the people and groups without self-discipline that are the most stressed and unprepared. Relax and stay mindful of how you use your time and energy.

5. **Take action.** Once you release your stress go into action mode, you can enjoy the feeling of accomplishment. You will discover that it is easier than you thought, and once you get started, you won't want to stop.

6. **Sharpen your focus.** Focus on the sense of accomplishment you will feel once you reach your goal. Create a strong connection to what you really want. A person or group with a burning desire is unstoppable.

7. **Prepare to succeed.** Get yourself organized. Make a schedule and stick with it. If you don't control your time, others will. Turn your vision into an action plan and have the self-discipline to work the plan. Break tasks down into manageable parts so that they don't seem overwhelming.

Create Your Own Self-Discipline Program

The best way to build more self-discipline is to do it gradually. Don't attempt to transform your life in one day. Much like progressive weight training, it's best to lift the amount closest to your limit, take a rest period, and then re-engage. If you attempt a weight that exceeds your maximum by too much, you could injure yourself and not be able to continue. On the other hand, if you lift weights that are well below your limit you won't put enough strain on your muscles to make progress. Find the right balance for yourself so that you can begin using and building your self-discipline muscle every day. Follow the steps below to get started.

1. **Take baby steps.** Start slow and track your progress. Crawl before you walk. You will notice yourself getting better.

2. **Do the most crucial assignments first.** Get in the habit of doing the highest priority task first instead of the most enjoyable. That way, even if you don't get everything done, you'll have completed the most crucial tasks.

3. **Track your progress.** Check in on how you're doing. Keep a tally of when you feel like you had a good self-discipline day and when you may have needed more.

4. **Stay engaged.** Create a strategy to remain focused and inspired. (Refer to your vision board; use affirmations such as, "I have unwavering self-discipline.")

5. **Be a finisher.** When you start something, finish it rather than leaving it "almost done."

6. **Find support and accountability.** Find partners in your quest for self-discipline. Are there people who can help you be more disciplined? A spouse, partner, friend, teammate or someone in your Bamboo Circle?

Water The Bamboo: The 21-Day Self-Discipline Challenge

Research indicates it takes 21 days to form a new habit. Strengthen your self-discipline and willpower by taking on small tasks or engaging for short periods of time, then gradually increasing your efforts. For example, if you have a habit of being late to appointments, apply the 21-day challenge. Make it a point to arrive at work, appointments, and meetings on time or early. Assess the reasons you find yourself being late, such as:

- Do you over-commit or underestimate how long things will take?

- Are you leaving early enough?

- Are you organized?

- Do you value your time and respect others' time?

Then create actions that will address those reasons. By being on time for 21 days, you will increase your self-discipline muscle and demonstrate to yourself your capability for discipline and the positive impacts of that discipline. Once you've done that, move on to something that's a little more of a challenge, but still manageable. Find another area in which you feel stuck or could use a bit more discipline – say it's networking or finding new clients. Plan to make three calls a day or meet three new prospects for 21 days. You don't have to tackle the most intimidating call or meeting on day one. The goal is to build your self-discipline confidence.

Water The Bamboo: Time Assessment

For seven days, keep track of how you spend your time in 30-minute intervals. Do you regularly say yes to a lesser desire in sacrifice of a greater one? How much energy and time could you re-direct toward your bamboo by eliminating some of your seemingly harmless, but also fruitless, endeavors? Cutting just one 30-minute television show or Internet session out of your life per week will create *26 hours* per year that you could apply to something that really matters.

What Trait Is This?

I am your constant companion.

I am your greatest helper or heaviest burden.
I will push you onward or drag you down to failure.
I am completely at your command.

Half of the things you do you might as well turn over to me and I will do
them — quickly and correctly.

I am easily managed — you must be firm with me.
Show me exactly how you want something done and after a few lessons, I
will do it automatically.

I am the servant of great people,
and alas, of all failures as well.
Those who are great, I have made great.
Those who are failures, I have made failures.

I am not a machine, though
I work with the precision of a machine
plus the intelligence of a person.

You may run me for profit or run me for ruin —
it makes no difference to me.

Take me, train me, be firm with me, and
I will place the world at your feet.

Be easy with me and I will destroy you.

Who am I? I am Habit.

- Anonymous

Language

"I figured that if I said it enough, I would convince the world that I really was the greatest." ~ Muhammad Ali

Too often we go through our lives unconsciously, not giving much thought to the "little voice" in each of our heads. You know the voice I mean – the one that is constantly chattering, evaluating and judging. If you don't believe me, stop reading right now and listen: See? *That* voice! That little voice is a strong indicator of how you see yourself and the world.

Psychologists say that the average person has more than 60,000 thoughts a day, and seventy-five percent of those thoughts are negative. That's pretty frightening when you consider that what we say to ourselves shapes our thinking, our thinking frames what we believe, and what we believe determines our actions and therefore our reality. Just like the classic children's story, *The Little Engine That Could*, we can choose to support or defeat ourselves with our own inner dialogue.

When we're in a negative state, the little voice says things like "I can't," "I'm not smart enough," "If only…" or "It won't work." But when we're in a positive state, it uses affirming language – things like "I can," "I will," "This will work out," and "This is great!" To have a more affirming state we need to learn to control that little voice, to train it into a consistently positive state, even when we're not.

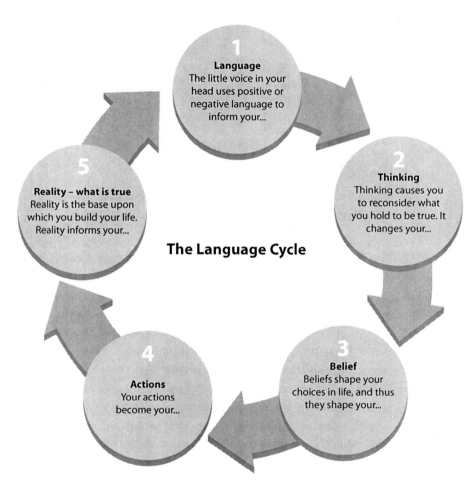

The Language Cycle

Language Changes What's True

In 1903, the record for running a mile was four minutes and 12.75 seconds. Harry Andrews, a British Olympic coach, stated that the record would never be broken. This declaration, and others like it, held back runners for years. Up until 1954, it was widely believed that breaking the four-minute mile was physically impossible. That year, Roger Bannister was the first man publicly acknowledged to break the four-minute mile. Shortly after, two more people did it, and the year after that, 236 people did! What do you think Bannister's little voice told him before he changed the reality of the day?

How is your self-talk stopping you in your life and your career? Is your little voice arguing for limitations with statements like "I'm too new here to make a difference," "This organization is dysfunctional," "Things will never change," "I'm too young or old," or "I'm just a... (secretary, custodian, middle manager, etc.)"? Perhaps it's time to change the little voice! When we do that, we change what we believe and open new doors of possibility. We also change how others perceive us because people believe what we project about ourselves.

Affirmations Work

Affirmations are a powerful and conscious way to guide the little voice. Because they are so simple and easy to use, most people underestimate their power. However, affirmations have been successfully used by medical patients, businesspeople, athletes, psychologists, and other successful people for centuries.

Program your language to affirm the person you want to be and the life you want to have. The key is to create short, positive statements about what you *want* to be true for yourself. Affirmations don't do it alone: Roger Bannister didn't break the record by just talking to himself. He trained day after day and did the hard work. Affirmations are the fuel that gets the train rolling. They give the crucial, and often most difficult, first push up that hill.

When we control our internal language, we create the reality that we want. Whether you are preparing for a new client meeting, a performance review, or a meeting with your business lender, if you use your language to help you envision a positive result, you are much more likely to succeed. With enough practice, you will find that your little voice automatically becomes more supportive and affirming of what you want.

Water The Bamboo: Notice Your Language

Make it a point to listen to your little voice over the next few days. What are you affirming? Is it what you want? Do you need to retrain your little voice? The two most critical times of your day are just after you wake up and just before you go to sleep. Our thoughts upon waking shape our belief about our prospects for the day. Our thoughts as we go to sleep inform our dreams. Note what your little voice is affirming at these important times. Consider how those thoughts may be shaping your outlook and your reality.

Water The Bamboo: Train Your Voice

Since everyone is unique, create your own affirmations tailored to fit you and your circumstances. Choose something you're struggling with and find a short, positive way to state what you want to be true. For example, if you find you are impatient with your coworkers or clients, you might script your affirmation this way: "I am patient and have positive interactions with colleagues." Formulate no more than three affirmations and write these in your journal.

Create some time alone and repeat your affirmations, either by saying or writing them, in the morning and at night at least 10 times at each sitting for 21 habit-forming days. After 21 days, ask yourself: What did I notice? How do I feel? Has anything changed?

Sample affirmations:

Self-Confidence

- "I am confident and positive."

- "I deserve to have success."

- "I am great at my work."

Financial Success

- "I am financially independent and secure."

- "I am prosperous."

Relationships and Client Service

- "I enjoy my time with my co-workers."

- "I like myself in the presence of others."

Communication

- "My communication is clear and effective."

- "I am a great listener."

Stress Reduction

- "I am calm and serene under pressure."

- "I feel relaxed."

Water The Bamboo: Convenient Reminder Card

Create an affirmation card. Write down your key affirmations on a card and place it in your wallet or purse or some other convenient location. Read the card while waiting in line or whenever you think of it.

Courage

"You gain strength, courage, and confidence by every experience in which you really stop to look fear in the face. You must do the thing which you think you cannot do." ~ *Eleanor Roosevelt*

The word for courage in Old French, "corage," is defined as "heart and spirit." It takes courage to go for what you want. Courage is having fear and acting anyway. To have success you must develop the ability to *not* let fear paralyze you. Focusing on fear *limits what is possible*. What if you went after your bamboo with all of your heart and spirit?

The energy you give to fear, when redirected, can be used on your bamboo instead. For example, you're scheduled to teach a new class tomorrow and you're full of anxiety. You could focus on your fear and spend your time worrying about how the group might not like you or what you have to say. What if, instead, you spent that time and energy learning about the audience, reviewing your notes, practicing your material with a supportive colleague or anticipating questions the audience might ask and outlining your responses? The latter approach is much more likely to help you avoid the thing you're probably afraid of – mistakes, embarrassment or seeming like you don't know what you're doing.

Stretch Your "Courage Zone"

The stronger your courage is, the more willing you will be to confront or engage in the numerous challenges you face as you go for your bamboo. Courage is the quality that allows you to stand up, look your fear in the face, and continue to move toward success.

In what areas of your life do you need to stretch your courage? For example, do you need to:

- speak up?
- do the right thing?
- do the unpopular thing?
- participate?

Courage can help you:

- express your ideas and thoughts
- lead your team in a different direction
- learn new skills
- share information
- be your authentic self
- make decisions with limited information

The First Step: Recall Your Courageous Acts

Your past acts of courage can give you strength today. Think of a time when you were afraid but acted anyway. What happened? Was it as bad as you imagined? Did you get unexpected support?

The Next Step: Find a Courageous Role Model

Think of someone who has exhibited courage. What did they do? What qualities do they have? Take on those qualities as your own. Role models can give you the strength to be more courageous – to say to yourself, "If they can have courage under those circumstances, why not me?" Courage is not reserved just for firefighters and soldiers. It serves the seemingly ordinary person who shows fearlessness daily without fanfare: the person who enters the workforce for the first time in years, the grandparent who goes back to complete a college degree or the person who volunteers for a complicated project.

The Last Step: Understand That Courage is an Action, Not a Personality Trait

A person's actions may be courageous, but it doesn't mean he or she is always courageous. The danger with attributing courage to personality, rather than an action, is that it suggests you either have it or you don't. In fact, every one of us has done something courageous at some point. You may have more courage in one area of your life than another. Courage in this context simply means taking action that moves you closer to your bamboo, even though you are scared, nervous or anxious.

There is a difference between courage and recklessness. There are real dangers that must be avoided, and courage is only effective when it is used to improve a situation. Recklessness won't get you closer to your bamboo.

Courage can lead you to make better choices – rather than simply taking the least difficult path – and can help you overcome criticism, fear and doubt as you plow into new endeavors.

Water The Bamboo: Building Courage

Start with small acts of courage to build up to bigger ones. For example, volunteer to do a section of the all-employee meeting before leading the whole project.

1. List the areas where you need to have more courage to achieve your bamboo.

2. Once you've got your list, number them in order of most challenging to least challenging for you.

3. Start at the least challenging and work your way up the list.

4. What stops you from being more courageous with each item?

    a. What would courage look and feel like?

    b. What is the first step?

    c. When will you start?

Bamboo Rule: The highest form of courage is to be true to yourself.

Appreciation

"What you appreciate appreciates." ~ *Lynne Twist, author*

Appreciation and gratitude are rare. When was the last time someone gave you genuine and specific appreciation? How did it make you feel? When was the last time you expressed such appreciation to someone else?

On a daily basis, people go above and beyond for others, often without an ounce of recognition or appreciation. Waiting around for a compliment can make you cynical and bitter. Instead, remind yourself to be appreciative and to model appreciation for others. You will notice those around you picking up on this simple but effective approach – both in terms of appreciating themselves and expressing their appreciation of others.

Bamboo Rule: Take time to genuinely appreciate the people in your life; don't wait for performance reviews or funerals.

Too often people feel ignored and underappreciated which can cause frustration, poor performance, less effort and low productivity. But don't despair. Regular, genuine appreciation with peers and clients can help energize the group: almost everyone is looking for some acknowledgment that they are making a difference. When they get noticed the results can be amazing.

Questions to Cultivate Appreciation

1. What is already working well for our group or team?
2. Who do we need to appreciate for what's working well?
3. What are our greatest strengths?
4. What systems and processes are particularly helpful?

Appreciation has magical benefits. It can foster:

- confidence and creativity
- dedication and a desire to go the extra mile
- loyalty and trust
- more effective relationships and group dynamics

Sincere appreciation motivates. It works both internally – when you take time to recognize what you appreciate about yourself or your situation – and externally – when you appreciate others and model appreciation for your team's strengths and accomplishments. Appreciation takes active looking and an expectation that things worth notice are happening all around.

As you're watering your bamboo, seek to share appreciation with others. Pay more attention to what you're focusing on and make appreciative questions part of your daily internal and external dialogue. A small, thoughtful expression of recognition and appreciation can be the seed that makes a big difference – in your life and in the lives of others.

Tips for Appreciation:

1. **You must be the driving force.** Don't rely on others to create appreciation in your work or home environment. You must set the tone, lead by example and continuously demonstrate appreciation with your own efforts and with your friends and co-workers, especially where others don't.

2. **Be authentic.** One of the worst things you can do is fake appreciation. People can smell it a mile away. Don't try to manipulate with empty words. If you tell people how much you value and appreciate them but don't mean a word of it, they will sense it and feel frustrated rather than motivated or valued.

3. **Acknowledge people directly and specifically.** A simple thing like saying hello using a person's name makes him or her feel valued. So imagine how much impact a thoughtful, genuine gesture of personalized appreciation can have. Tell people exactly what you appreciate about them or what they did.

4. **Be consistent, but don't use the same methods for everyone.** Find out how individuals like to be appreciated (for example, private, handwritten notes for some and verbal, public appreciation for others).

5. **Go beyond pre-defined "appreciation times" such as Administrative Assistants' Day, birthdays, or annual reviews.** Holiday appreciations are fine, but don't let it be the only time you show appreciation. Celebrating a person for one day and ignoring them the rest of the year is counter-productive. It can seem like an obligation instead of a genuine appreciation. Appreciate people consistently throughout the year. Don't assume they know they are appreciated.

6. **Don't let an opportunity to show appreciation pass.** Don't wait for the "perfect time" to express gratitude. If someone does something meaningful, let them know as soon as possible. Even if you forget at the time, don't give up. Instead, go back and say, "I missed an opportunity earlier to say thank you for _____." Keep thank-you notes handy so that you can show appreciation right away. Schedule a time each day or week to think about and write to the people you appreciate.

7. **Don't overdo it.** If all you ever do is praise, your appreciation will begin to ring hollow. Appreciating people doesn't mean you never offer them constructive feedback, either. In fact, sincere appreciation and well-delivered, constructive feedback actually complement each other by communicating that you are paying attention to the other person and are sincere in your feedback to them.

8. **Practice, practice, practice.** If appreciation is not something that you normally do, start practicing at home with your family, partner or children and then integrate the practice at work. Try it out as an experiment and notice what happens.

9. **Appreciate yourself too.** Don't underestimate the value of appreciating yourself for the things you do for others and for yourself.

Use appreciation as an ongoing motivator for yourself and others. Think of it as a type of energy, much like electricity. You will find that it has an enormous and reliable impact on what happens in your business and in your life.

Water The Bamboo: Cultivate Appreciation

Write down three things you could do to bring more appreciation to your work and personal life.

Lighten Up

"Humor is mankind's greatest blessing." ~ *Mark Twain*

Your ability to lighten up and maintain your sense of fun and humor – despite the pressures of life and work – can determine the quality of your experience, your ideas, your health and your accomplishments.

Bamboo Rule: Choose your lines wisely: frown lines or smile lines.

Humor Fertilizes Creativity and Health

Playfulness and humor improve the quality of a person's ideas and creativity, not to mention a person's health. An environment that supports playfulness and lightness can lead to an increase in resourcefulness and creativity. Studies have shown that laughter reduces stress hormones and increases the level of mood- and health-enhancing chemicals such as endorphins and dopamine.

Warning signs you may need to lighten up:

- Everything is your fault

- Everything is someone else's fault

- You spend more time worrying about things you can't control than taking action on things you can control

- You get angry and frustrated easily or have "meltdowns" on a regular basis

- You laugh infrequently

Five Ways to Start Lightening Up:

1. **Identify the kinds of things that cause you stress.** Are there any underlying issues that you haven't addressed? How might you be able to get support to address those issues? Are you overscheduled or unrealistic about how long it takes to do something or get somewhere? Work on scheduling less, so you're not constantly running from one thing to the next. Pad your tasks so you have some cushion if something unexpected happens. You might even have time to take a few deep breaths and relax. With a little focus and effort, you can unburden yourself of some of your stress and enjoy life more.

2. **Don't take yourself, or your daily struggles, too seriously.** When things go wrong, ask yourself, "Will this matter tomorrow? A week from now? Next year?" If not, it's probably not worth worrying over now. Give yourself permission to laugh and move on.

3. **Pursue excellence rather than perfection.** Unlike gymnastics and figure skating, there is no clear definition of perfection in the professional realm. Excellence doesn't mean that you're sacrificing quality, but you're also not sacrificing your soul. It allows for mistakes

and humanity but still aims for great results. Addressing mistakes with good humor and an attitude of learning is an indication that you're pursuing excellence, not perfection.

4. **Practice instant forgiveness.** People, including you, make mistakes, so why not forgive them as soon as the mistake is made? Gallup research indicates that 97% of people believe in forgiveness, but only 47% of the population regularly forgives others. Obviously, it's a pretty hard thing to do. But the irony of forgiveness is it helps the "victim" most of all. Once you forgive, you no longer carry anger or resentment – leaving you light and ready for your next activity.

Bamboo Rule: The first person to forgive is yourself.

5. **Lighten up your environment: get rid of clutter.** Be brutal about getting rid of things that can accumulate in your workspace or home; if you don't love it or need it, get rid of it. Keeping useless things around only makes it harder to see the things that are important to you because you're moving the useless things from here to there. It's hard to be "light" when you feel burdened by clutter. Did you know that the average executive spends an astonishing six weeks a year looking for lost items at the office? Given that you'll never look at 80% of the paper you have again – it's clearly hard to be your most effective under clutter – keep that recycling bin nearby and toss what you don't need.

Have Fun with Each Other

Teams that figure out how to integrate humor and fun into their work culture differentiate themselves with greater employee satisfaction, health, creativity and retention.

Bamboo Rule: Focus on having fun, not being funny.

Bamboo Example: *Fun doesn't have to be confetti and balloons. It can be as unconventional (and fuzzy) as the slippers worn by managers at the Quality Suites Hotel behind Busch Gardens in Tampa, Florida. Owner John Ruzic saw the value of fun when he got into a confrontation with an employee, glimpsed the man's Scooby Doo footwear and dissolved into gales of laughter. "When two parties are wearing Tasmanian Devil or skunk slippers, there's no way they can get upset," says Ruzic. "It completely takes the anger out of the workplace."*

(From "Mixing Business and Pleasure is No Longer Taboo" by Michelle Prather and David Doran, Entrepreneur, July 1999.)

Humor Etiquette

Avoid hateful humor or making fun of people based on their social status – race, gender, religion, age, size – and limit sarcasm.

Positive Humor	**Negative Humor**
• Bonds people	• Divides people
• Releases stress	• Causes tension
• Includes laughing at self	• Focuses on laughing at others

Bamboo Rule: Take your work seriously,
but don't take yourself seriously.

Only You Can Prevent the Loss of Your Sense of Humor

You can still lighten up whether or not your organization sets a humorous tone. One way to do it is to embrace the playful nature of the child in you. Children laugh on average 415 times a day; adults average only 15. You too were a child once, so start being generous with your laughter – your friends, family and co-workers will love you for it!

An atmosphere that is more playful and humorous is one that employees like to be a part of. People who view their work as fun are more productive and creative than those who are merely satisfied with their jobs. And most importantly, creating an environment where people can be light and have fun with each other can lead to a culture where valuable connections between colleagues and departments are formed.

Water The Bamboo: Don't Wait to Lighten Up

- What can you do in the next 24 hours to lighten up? How can you expand that one action into a regular pattern?

- Regularly schedule time to clear the clutter from your home, workspace and computer.

- Eliminate pet projects or things that are not central to your bamboo or your values.

twelve

Optimism

"Everything can be taken from a man but one thing; the last of human freedoms – to choose one's attitude in any given set of circumstances, to choose one's own way." ~ Viktor Frankl

Optimism helps you cope with the daily grind and the inevitable challenges you will face as you water your bamboo. It is a state of mind that is well worth developing and strengthening. Aside from just making you feel better, being optimistic:

- trains you to be solution-oriented

- helps you to expect the best from people and situations

- reduces stress and increases joy

- improves your relationships

- helps you see more opportunities

Optimism is also contagious. Have you ever been around someone who is genuinely optimistic? How did you feel?

Bamboo Rule: Successful people don't have pity parties.

Successful people face many of the same challenges that less prosperous and satisfied people do. The difference lies largely in how they choose to respond to those challenges. A study of history's 300 greatest leaders – including Abraham Lincoln, Dr. Martin Luther King, Jr., Helen Keller, Mother Teresa, and Franklin D. Roosevelt – showed that three-fourths of them came from "disadvantaged" backgrounds. Despite the challenges they faced, they remained optimistic.

What's Your Approach?

Consider this: There are multiple ways to look at the same situation.

The pessimistic approach says: This is what is wrong and there is nothing we can do about it. The optimistic approach says: This is what is going well and this is what we are going to do about our challenges. Which approach do you think is more likely to lead to solutions and success? Which approach do you want for yourself and your team?

Bamboo Rule: Attitude is a choice.

The answer to the age old question, "Is the glass half empty or half full?" is that *it's both.* The real question is, which do you emphasize – what you have or what you don't have? Adopting a half-full perspective does not mean you ignore challenges or bury your head in the sand. Instead, it reminds you to focus on what you have and motivates you to handle the challenges that come your way.

> ***Bamboo Example:*** *Johnny and Bobby are twins. Johnny is extremely optimistic and Bobby extremely pessimistic. Their parents are concerned about both of them. For their birthday, the parents decided to try and balance this out. They give Bobby a room full of*

candy, toys and games and Johnny a room filled with horse manure. When they check on them in their respective rooms, they find Bobby complaining about everything: "The candy's too sweet, this toy is too loud, I don't like this color," and so on. The parents think their experiment is a disaster. They go to check on Johnny. When they peek through the window they see Johnny with his shirt off, sweating, and shoveling manure everywhere. His parents push the door open and say, "Johnny, what are you doing?" Johnny replies, "With all this manure, there has to be a pony in here somewhere!" Now that's optimism.

Start looking for ponies in your life. Today and in the future choose to focus on what you have and look for what you want to see. Start each day by asking yourself and others a very simple and optimistic question: "What's going well?" Do it right now. Write down three things that are going well, either personally or professionally. Notice how this shifts your mood. When you look for what's going well, you'll see it.

"The point of living, and of being an optimist, is to be foolish enough to believe the best is yet to come." ~ Peter Ustinov

Maintaining an Optimistic Attitude in the Face of "Negaholics"

Some people just cannot visualize success for themselves or other people, and they spread their pessimism whenever they can. These "negaholics," are overly cynical and disparaging to others. They focus on the negative, and most have been practicing for a long time and have become "experts." They also love company, and do their best to suck other people into their negative mind-set.

You can usually tell whether someone is a "negaholic" by considering how you feel when you are with him or her. Are they consistently starting pity parties? Do you leave them feeling drained and depleted?

Many people struggle with at least one "negaholic" at work or in their personal lives, and they want to know how to deal with that person. Here are a few suggestions:

Leave negative situations. It's not your job to talk people out of their pessimism or try to make them feel better. Your goal is to deflect negativity, not rid the world of it. Be true to yourself when dealing with the "negaholic." Excuse yourself from the situation by simply saying, "I have a commitment I need to take care of." You would be careful of exposure to germs if a friend had the flu. The same should be true of the person spreading unwanted negativity.

Invite the "negaholic" to take some responsibility. Ask:

- "What are you planning to do about it?"
- "What's one thing you can do to improve the situation?"

Strengthen and protect your professional and personal boundaries. Make your boundaries clear in terms of negativity – what is okay with you and what's not? Then, clearly and compassionately state your boundaries to the "negaholic," or excuse yourself when the conversation starts to head in a negative direction. You're not required to be an audience.

Water The Bamboo: Optimistic Monday

Create an entire day dedicated to optimism – call it Optimistic Monday or another name of your choosing. The objective is to be over-the-top optimistic – much like Johnny in the previous Bamboo Example. As challenges come up, consciously choose to see the glass half full. Highlight the positive whenever possible. At the end of the day, reflect on what you noticed during the day. How did you feel? What were your interactions like with colleagues and friends?

The Optimist Creed

Promise Yourself …

- to be so strong that nothing can disturb your peace of mind
- to talk health, happiness, and prosperity to every person you meet
- to make all your friends feel that there is something worthwhile in them
- to look at the sunny side of everything and make your optimism come true
- to think only of the best, to work only for the best and to expect only the best
- to be just as enthusiastic about the success of others as you are about your own
- to forget the mistakes of the past and press on to the greater achievements of the future
- to wear a cheerful expression at all times and give a smile to every living creature you meet
- to give so much time to improving yourself that you have no time to criticize others
- to be too large for worry, too noble for anger, too strong for fear, and too happy to permit the presence of trouble
- to think well of yourself and to proclaim this fact to the world, not in loud word, but in great deeds
- to live in the faith that the whole world is on your side, so long as you are true to the best that is in you

Adapted from Christian D. Larson and Optimist International

Read and reread this creed and commit it to memory…better yet, commit it to practice!

PREPARE THE SOIL

thirteen

Learn How to Learn

"In times of change learners inherit the earth while the learned find themselves beautifully equipped to work in a world that no longer exists." ~ Eric Hoffer, author

Learning how to learn has never been more critical than today. The world is changing so rapidly that you can't afford not to be a learner – there's not much in the world that doesn't become outdated in a short time. Without a conscious, active learning plan you will soon be outpaced by your colleagues and competitors.

Be Eager to Learn

The root of the word student is the Latin word *studiere*, which means simply, "eager to learn." It doesn't mean you're in a classroom or some formal setting, it just means you're willing to learn. That willingness not only opens you for learning, but exposes you to *opportunities* for learning.

*Bamboo Rule: A side benefit of growing bamboo is
the education that you gain along the way.*

When you set out to learn – which should be a continuous endeavor for all bamboo farmers – consider the mood, attitude, and willingness you're bringing to the effort. Do you have an open mind? Do you understand the value and expertise others bring to the world? Are you willing to let others contribute to you? As you work the exercises in this book, as you learn any new skill at work, and as you're talking to strangers at the grocery store, keep an eagerness to learn, a sponge-like quality that will help you absorb new clues and new information about people and the world around you. Your eagerness will make a difference in what you take away, and it's also a good practice to keep yourself open to new thoughts, new information, and new approaches.

Levels of Learning

As you go through the learning process with anything, it's helpful to understand the four levels of learning, based on a model by communication skills pioneer Dr. Thomas Gordon. What level are you currently in with a particular skill?

Level 1: Unconscious Incompetence. You're unaware of what you don't know – both in terms of deficit in skill or knowledge you don't currently possess.

Level 2: Conscious Incompetence. You know what you don't know. Here, you recognize the deficit of what you don't know, and you're motivated to learn.

Level 3: Conscious Competence. You know what you know – you are aware of the skills and knowledge you have gained and are ready to accomplish something. However, demonstrating the skill or knowledge requires a great deal of awareness and focus.

Level 4: Unconscious Competence. You don't have to think about what you know – you have had so much practice with a skill that it becomes second nature and can be performed easily (often without concentrating too deeply). You can also teach the skill to others.

What is Your Learning Style?

Everyone may go through the same levels of learning, but everyone has a different learning *style*. Researchers commonly identify four prominent learning styles:

1. **Visual** learners prefer seeing what they are learning.

2. **Auditory** learners prefer spoken messages, either someone else's voice or their own.

3. **Kinesthetic** learners want to sense the position and movement of what they are working on.

4. **Tactile** learners want to touch and "get their hands dirty."

You can make learning easier by honoring your unique learning style. There is a lot of research out there; a simple Internet search on "learning styles" will produce multiple self-tests you can use to determine your particular style. And remember, teachers often assume their students learn the same way they do; consequently, they teach the way they would want to receive information. You have a role in helping your teacher, guide or mentor understand your learning style and how you best take in information. If you're teaching a group, ask your students how they learn best.

The Learning Process

Interestingly, no matter what your learning style is or what stage of learning you're in, all of us go through the following steps in the learning process (adapted from work by Malcolm Knowles and Peter Senge).

What's In It for Me?

Early on in the learning process, ask yourself, "What's in it for me? How is this relevant to my bamboo?" You will be more engaged in the learning once you have identified the relevance of the learning.

Step 1: Humility. Admit you don't know all that is necessary for success. Being open to new information is the first step in learning.

Step 2: Intake. Allow the information others have to offer to enter into your mind. Whether you're a manager, employee, teacher, student, or mentor, it is important to create a safe learning environment, where mistakes are allowed and "re-dos" are encouraged.

Bamboo Rule: Get it right the third time.

Step 3: Clarity with repetition. Learning is a dynamic process, where student and teacher work together to reach clarity about what's being taught. In either role, make room for dialogue or conversation about the information being shared. If you're the student, repeat what you understand and ask for confirmation: "Is that right?" If you're the teacher, ask your student to tell you in their own words what they understand. The more you repeat and review the learning, the better you know how to do it.

Step 4: Application. Once you know how to do something through intake and repetition, you can consciously apply what you've learned in a real situation. This is the difference between simply mirroring or role playing something and actually putting it to use. This concept is covered in depth in the next chapter, "Practice Deliberately."

Step 5: Internalization. Internalization is where you're not really thinking about the activity, you're simply doing it. There are things that you have internalized, like driving your car or riding your bike. Until you internalized the skill, you had to think about all the mechanics that now seem natural.

Learning Tips:

- Learn a little at a time
- Set time to review what you have learned
- Teach to others because the teacher is the learner
- Keep a journal

Bamboo Rule: Impatience is the enemy of mastery.

Water The Bamboo: Start Learning!

1. List three things you need to learn more about or three skills you need to develop or improve in order to grow your bamboo.

2. For each one, identify three approaches to learning more about it – whether it's reading a monthly periodical, doing research, setting up a relationship with a mentor or taking a class.

3. Create a learning plan for each of these three areas for the next year. Maybe you're going to set an evening aside each month to read a business or trade magazine, you're going to attend a conference and meet once per quarter with your mentor. Set goals to help you measure your progress. Are you actually retaining anything from that magazine? Is the conference worthwhile? Make sure your learning time is well spent.

fourteen

Practice Deliberately

"Deliberate practice is about changing your performance, setting new goals and straining yourself to reach a bit higher each time. It involves you deciding to improve something and setting up training conditions to attain the skill." ~ Anders Ericsson, psychologist

Successful people and organizations have been quietly and deliberately watering their bamboo for years before they become household names. Superior performers have two things in common – unrelenting diligence and the willingness to practice intensely. This idea has been underscored by researchers studying top achievers across a variety of disciplines: successful people employ what's called "deliberate practice" to get where they want to be.

Deliberate practice is different from any other practice. It's a *systematic* form of practice designed to improve performance. It pushes you beyond your comfort zone, provides feedback on outcomes, and involves lots of repetition.

Most people practice in the same way they've always performed a skill. In other words, they practice the same motions, the same steps, the same process, over and over again, hoping it will improve by sheer repetition. For example, a basketball player practices a three-point shot by making the same shot hundreds of times. Deliberate practice is different – it involves working on an aspect of the skill you want that's a little bit outside of what you already know. It also requires you to simulate real-life conditions as much as possible, and gather specific feedback on your performance. So now, that same basketball player is practicing the shot with a defender contesting his shot. He has also piped in crowd noise to simulate a real game, and he's evaluating his performance through a coach or by videotaping his shots. As with any practice, much of this hard work and practice happens when no one is watching but that supportive and skilled coach or mentor.

World-class achievers employ deliberate practice. The best person or organization in their field is deliberately practicing right now. They are working on a skill they don't quite have yet. They are probably getting some good coaching that includes critical feedback. They are doing this countless times, from a variety of angles, until they get it right. And you and your team can, too.

The Ten-Year Rule

The good news is that successful people are made, not born. Success is the byproduct of years of focused practice and experience rather than some innate gift or talent. The hard news is there are no short cuts. It takes at least 10 years of deliberate practice to become a master in any field. (Credit yourself for each year of your past relevant experience.) To become successful, you must:

- invest your time wisely – roughly three hours per day for 10 years

- practice beyond your current comfort level

- work with a well-informed coach who can give support and critical feedback

Countless examples of those thought to be "naturals" in their fields owe the majority of their success to a decade of deliberate practice. By the time he was crowned chess grandmaster, Bobby Fischer had practiced for nine of his 16 years. Before winning the 1976 Olympics, Nadia Comaneci, triple gold-medal gymnast at age 14, had practiced under superior coaching since she was in kindergarten. There is no Mozart exception either. Often presented as the classic child prodigy with exceptional, innate musical ability, Wolfgang Amadeus Mozart started deliberate practice prior to age four. His father – a composer, famous music teacher, and author of what is believed to be one of the first books on violin instruction – ensured his son's natural talent would blossom through the discipline of hard work and deliberate practice. Like other successful people Mozart wasn't born a master – he became one.

Just as with athletes, composers and chess champions, there are many opportunities to apply the laws of deliberate practice to business: it works on any improvable skill, be it listening, communicating, teaching, negotiating, accounting, presenting, managing people and more. The key is to approach these skills with a desire to improve rather than just getting your work done. Those who practice deliberately are better able to handle the uncontrollable variables such as competitors, the economy, colleagues, and clients.

> ***Bamboo Example:*** *Take the rookie analyst: years ago someone advised her to work on her presentation skills because she was terrified to speak in front of groups. She reluctantly joined Toastmasters, hired a speaking coach, volunteered to present at conferences and practiced for years under her coach. One day she was asked to stand in at the last minute for a colleague and present to the organization's leadership team. She wowed her audience with her command of the material, her clarity and her organization – all skills she developed through deliberate practice. Soon after she received a promotion. Little did they know she had been deliberately practicing for that moment for years.*

Bamboo Rule: Success happens when no one is watching.

Water The Bamboo: How to Practice Deliberate Practice

1. **Identify a weakness you want to improve.** Resist the temptation to work on only what you have mastered. Ideally, the skill you work on should be connected to some part of your bamboo – your vision or one of the goals that will get you there.

2. **Research.** Start by researching the skill you want to master. Look for experts in your area, interview them, and take classes. Learn as much as you can.

3. **Find a coach.** Seek help from someone who is great at the skill you wish to acquire and has a proven track record as a coach. Great coaching and support can accelerate your growth. Find someone in your organization who has mastery in a skill you want to develop and ask for his or her help. Good coaches can see your blind spots and provide critical information you will need in order to improve. You want feedback now when you're in practice mode, rather than later when it's time to perform.

4. **Design a Practice Plan.** Develop your plan and track your progress. Early morning is a good time to practice, or whenever you are most alert and ready.

Bamboo Rule: Practice makes permanent.

Stay Motivated After You Plateau

When most people practice, they improve at first, and then the rate of return on their practice slows and they plateau. That's the point at which many people stop working because the improvement seems so slight relative to the results they saw in the beginning. Mastery requires that you push beyond the plateau, practicing as diligently and as specifically as ever. Even though you're not seeing growth right now, have faith that the incremental improvement is vital to success.

Get practicing so that you can start growing!

It's Messy in the Garden

"Beginnings are always messy" ~ John Galsworthy, Nobel laureate

You can't plant a garden – bamboo or otherwise – without getting at least a little dirty. The most spectacular gardens in the world (Butchart Gardens in British Columbia; Keukenhof Gardens in Holland; a neighbor's you admire) are often big piles of dirt, rocks and sticks to start with – and they're constantly being dug into, rearranged, weeded, and otherwise messed up and muddied. But all that happens *behind* the scenes. When guests come, the gardens are pristine. You don't see the mess; you see the results.

Bamboo Rule: Don't take your mess from the garden to the living room.

That mess is inherent to any major endeavor. It's part of growing bamboo or getting any project off the ground. But many of us are surprised and discouraged when things are chaotic. We expect to be able to do big things without making a mess. Have you ever been in the kitchen of your favorite restaurant? My guess is it's absolutely chaotic at peak time – noisy, hot, with spills everywhere. But out in the dining room, all is calm, orderly, clean and elegant.

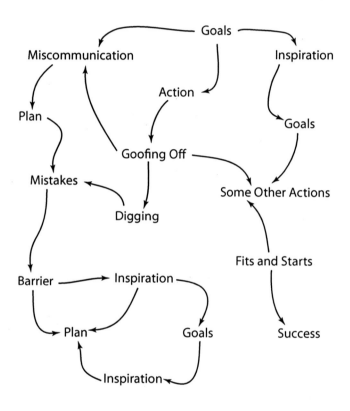

To have success, you must put up with some disorder; it rarely occurs in a linear path.

What in your life or your work so far has gone exactly as planned? Major clients leave, co-workers find other opportunities, deadlines are missed. It's all messy. The world and people are too complex for it not to be. Of course, when you hear about successful organizations and people, you rarely hear about the messes they experienced. You hear about what they created. Successful people and teams focus on the final product – the bamboo, the finished garden.

> **Bamboo Example:** *Frederick W. Smith, founder of Federal Express, made huge messes as he was building his company – right from the start. The company's launch, serving 11 cities, boasted only seven deliveries on its first night. Smith expanded his network, sent his sales force back into the field, and launched again, this time with more than 25 times as many packages.*
>
> *But more messes awaited. At one point, though he had started with a $4 million inheritance and $80 million more from venture capitalists, his organization was financially teetering and he couldn't make payroll. His solution? Vegas. As the story goes, Smith made $27,000 at the blackjack tables, wired the money back to his company, and kept it afloat long enough for it to survive – and thrive – on its own. Now that's messy.*

In order to grow bamboo, you've got to plant the seed in the ground. You've got to dig up a lot of dirt. If it rains, you're going to have mud. You'll hit rocks and may even chip your shovel. All of this is part of getting messy. Individuals and organizations need to adopt a messy-garden mindset. If you stifle the initial sloppiness, you risk stunting progress. If you're afraid of the sloppiness, you may never even start, or you won't allow time for your messes.

But if you're expecting the messiness, its inevitable arrival won't faze or discourage you. You'll recognize the messes for what they are – part of the normal growth process – and you'll have more faith in carrying on.

Keep in mind, however, that in your messy garden, what you *don't* want is chaos without purpose. You'll be doing a fair amount of weeding to get rid of unwanted clutter and obstacles to growth. Are you putting your energy into what matters most to you – your bamboo? Or are you growing a lot of dandelions too?

Bamboo Rule: Don't let the weeds grow higher than your bamboo.

You don't have to show your messes to your clients, your colleagues, or your co-workers. There's value in digging deeply in the garden but cleaning up before your guests arrive. People don't need to know about all the chaos it took to successfully complete the project. Your coworkers and clients don't need to hear about your messes.

As you're tending your bamboo, expect it to be a little bit rough. Embrace the dirt under your fingernails and the mud on your face as badges of the action you're taking. And keep digging and watering. You'll have time to clean up later.

Water The Bamboo: Your Messy Past

Think of past projects or experiences where you've had success. It's likely there was some element that was messy. What was it? Where have you allowed things to get messy in the past? How did you handle it? Were you able to rise above the mess and stay focused on your ultimate goal? What lessons can you extract from your past experiences?

PLANT THE SEED

Take Risks

"Avoiding danger is no safer in the long run than outright exposure. Life is either a daring adventure or nothing." ~ Helen Keller

I f you've had any success in your life, it is because you took risk. Risk is the predecessor to all successes, big or small. Look around and you'll see that successful people are the greatest risk takers. Risk is about stretching beyond your comfort zone and learning what you're made of. Risk is about tapping your potential for all it's worth. Only by doing this can you grow. To have the bamboo you want, you have to rediscover your ability to take risks!

Bamboo Rule: The turtle only moves when it sticks its neck out.

While risk involves danger, tension and potential loss, taking risks is part of business and life. Risk has a positive side too; it offers the ingredient for and chance of being successful.

We all were born with the ability to take risks. However, well-intending adults looking out for our safety repeatedly warned us to "be careful," or to "get down from there." Consequently, we carry into adulthood a fear of being hurt that can impede our ability to take the risk necessary to succeed; what served us well as kids becomes a detriment as adults.

The average child falls at least 200 times, bumping his head on coffee tables and scraping knees, before finally learning how to cross a room on two feet. Fast forward a couple of decades: though we instinctively understand that there is no progress without risk, we fall into the habit of avoiding risk.

Don't take risks just for risk's sake. The risk has to be worth it. Taking risks has two important potential rewards: the first is what you may gain if your risk pays off – a better job, a new client, a new relationship, the success of a new venture. Secondly, risk *will* pay off in terms of how you view yourself: you'll feel a sense of confidence, excitement, achievement and vigor. It is truly a win-win situation; even if the attempt "fails," you'll have gained valuable information from the attempt so that you can refine and risk again – this time with more knowledge.

> *Bamboo Rule: Take intelligent risks – not every risk is the "right" risk.*

There is rarely, if ever, a perfect time to "go for it," and delaying action usually won't guarantee any less risk. *Action* is what separates someone with a great *plan* from someone with a great *accomplishment.* Any thoughtful attempt is better than the perfect plan that's never tried.

Start Small

Set yourself up to succeed. You wouldn't ask a beginning driver to take the freeway or a new lawyer to handle a complex case. Smart people and organizations test their ideas sometimes for years before the full launch. Pilot your idea. Incubate your idea before you expose it to the world – just not for too long. Get it almost ready, and then seek feedback. That may turn out to be your first risk: putting your idea in front of others and asking for honest input.

Sometimes the best thing you can do with a project you have been working on is to share a draft and listen to the feedback. The feedback will help you improve your idea and can help you ultimately succeed.

Often, we hesitate to take action on our plans because we don't want to look foolish or unprepared. The key is to combine a thick skin with a long-term view of what you hope to accomplish. You may look foolish – everyone does in the beginning. The important thing is to begin, learn from the feedback, refine, and keep tending your bamboo. You have to start failing so you can start succeeding.

> *"Only those who risk going too far can possibly find out how far they can go." ~ T.S. Eliot, poet*

There Is No Box

Historically speaking, we often discover that "facts" are nothing more than the erroneous beliefs of the time (the world is flat, the sun rotates around the earth, you can't run a four-minute mile, a machine can't stay in the sky). These all have been proven wrong by risk takers. Many of the things we believe to be true today will eventually be proven false. By taking a risk, you could be the next person to create or change history!

Test the Boundaries of Your Comfort Zone

- Your comfort zone = where you are
- Your empowerment zone = where you want to go

What risk do you have to take to get you where you want to go? Learn new skills, develop relationships, plant the seed, make a change.

Water The Bamboo: Steps to Taking Risk

1. Identify the risk. What kind of risk is it? Does it threaten your financial, physical or emotional safety? If so, how? What can you do to reduce the threat?

2. Identify risks you've taken that turned out well.

3. Conduct research. Interview others who are successful.

4. Take baby steps. Start out with the smallest risk that will take you closer to where you want to be. Once you've experienced that and learned from it, move on.

5. Get support. Where can you get support in dealing with the situation so that you can take action? Ideally, join or form a Bamboo Circle.

seventeen

Commit to Your Bamboo

"Unless commitment is made, there are only promises and hopes; but no plans." ~ Peter F. Drucker

In order to achieve success in anything in life, you must commit to hard work. It takes unwavering commitment to whatever is necessary to successfully grow your bamboo. As the saying goes, if it were easy anyone would do it.

Bamboo Rule: Success comes with the commitment to "burn the ships."

In 1519 Spanish explorer Hernán Cortez sailed his fleet of ships into the harbor of Veracruz, Mexico. It was common practice in those days to leave guards with the ships, as they might be needed later to speed a retreat from the enemy. Cortez didn't want to leave any doubts in his crews' mind about their mission, so he gave the order to "burn the ships." He was fully committed to the mission, eliminating the option of retreat.

117

Fully committing to success means there are no excuses, no holding back: you employ a "non-negotiable" approach to your goal. Commit to the steps necessary to fully grow your bamboo, then burn your boatloads of excuses. Nothing short of total realization of your plan is acceptable.

Once you've done away with excuses, you'll find it easier to stop sabotaging your success. No more reaching one foot forward, and – just in case things don't work out – keeping the other foot planted firmly on familiar and comfortable ground.

> *"Desire is the key to motivation, but it's determination and commitment to an unrelenting pursuit of your goal – a commitment to excellence – that will enable you to attain the success you seek." ~ Mario Andretti*

I Will

Commitment requires that you change the verb from *want* to *will*. I *will* contact new prospects this week. I *will* make this deadline. I *will* change my attitude. Full commitment also means eliminating, "woulda, coulda, shoulda," and "When I get around to it" from your vocabulary. It means owning what you want and devoting the resources required to accomplishing your vision.

> *Bamboo Rule: Commitment is the bridge between desire and accomplishment.*

Whatever your particular bamboo may be – whether it's strengthening relationships, learning a new system, changing careers, or moving away from unhealthy things or people – you will find that what you accomplish is equal to your level of commitment. Simply choosing to stay committed may turn out to be your greatest accomplishment in and of itself.

If you've faltered in your commitment to your bamboo, don't give up! If it's still important to you, find a way to recommit. Ask yourself:

- What exactly am I committed to?
- What am I willing to sacrifice in order to accomplish my goals?
- Is my goal realistic given my level of commitment?

Questions like these are useful tools for evaluating your level of commitment when setbacks strike or your passion wavers. Just as the bamboo farmer checks the sky to determine the weather, you too will need to check your internal almanac of shifting moods, priorities and desires.

> *"The quality of a person's life is in direct proportion to their commitment to excellence, regardless of their chosen field of endeavor." ~ Vince Lombardi*

Five Steps to Recommitment

1. **Evaluate what has changed.** Has your industry, product, or work changed? Have demands on your personal life increased? Are you bored? The source of your dissatisfaction greatly affects the solution you'll choose.

2. **Give yourself a recommitment goal.** Re-evaluate your initial goals, and revise as necessary. Set a challenging goal that, once accomplished, will validate that you're back on track.

3. **Develop a new action plan.** Establish a list of actions to take in recommitting yourself. These actions may be different than your original action list now that you've done some initial work, gotten feedback, or your circumstances have changed.

4. **Boost your motivation by exposing yourself to new ideas.** Go to training programs, lectures, seminars. Read industry publications.

No matter how skilled you are, you can learn more and improve. That knowledge and progress may be just what you need to nudge yourself back into total commitment.

5. **Get support.** Ask your teammates, colleagues, friends and family for the support you need to recommit and help you be accountable. Consider finding a coach to meet with on a regular basis.

Commitments to Yourself

How many times have you made a commitment to yourself only to say "I can do that tomorrow," and tomorrow becomes next week or perhaps never comes at all? If we don't honor these little commitments to ourselves, we might say "So what?" After all, only we know about them. We're not hurting anyone.

That, however, is not true. You're hurting the most important person there is: yourself. How much of your time on a daily basis is spent fighting with yourself over whether or not to keep your commitments or carry out your action plans? You promise yourself you will exercise in the morning and then you argue with yourself, "I was up late," "I'm tired," "I'll do it later," or "I need to get work done."

When you don't follow through on commitments you've made to yourself, you chip away at your self-confidence and self-respect. You lose faith in your ability to produce results. You weaken your sense of integrity.

When you *act* on your commitments, you reinforce to yourself that your words mean something. Once you've committed to it, that commitment will turn into action. The more you believe this about yourself, the more seriously you'll take your commitments, and therefore, the more powerful they will be.

Commitments to Others

Every time you don't keep a commitment you make to someone else, you lose their trust, respect and credibility, and again you erode your own sense of personal power. You may think breaking these little commitments is no big deal, but in fact they are a very big deal. When you don't do what you say you will, you create confusion and self-doubt in your unconscious mind, and you teach others you don't mean what you say.

Be Careful About Overcommitting

Are you one of those people who overcommits in the interest of pleasing people or being helpful? Maybe you just can't say no. In either case, think about the results when you cannot deliver, to your own mental energy and to others' perceptions of you. Don't commit to things you know you won't do. There is no "try" when it comes to commitment; you either do it or you don't.

Learn to prioritize and be realistic about what you can accomplish in a certain amount of time. Make sure you put yourself and your own needs high on the list. Then, keep your commitments and be surprised by how true commitment dramatically increases your personal satisfaction and the successes you achieve each day.

eighteen

Decisions, Decisions and More Decisions

"It's important to be intuitive, but not at the expense of facts." ~ Michael Dell, entrepreneur

L ife and business are all about making decisions. You are a product of the decisions you have made in your life to date. A series of decisions leads to outcomes that either grow your bamboo or cause it to wither. When you see a successful person or organization, you're looking at a person or group who has figured out a process for making courageous and effective decisions. When you have a decision to make, do you have an approach? Are you haphazard or do you follow a process?

Decision Defined

The Latin root of the word decision means, "to cut off from all alternatives." When making a decision, you are simply choosing among alternatives. Once you make a choice, you eliminate the others.

Decisiveness, followed by action, is a key trait distinguishing successful teams and individuals from average or low achievers. The world is largely unscripted; therefore, it is important that you learn how to make sound decisions.

Use Your Values to Guide Your Decisions

Abandoning politically correct and bureaucratic procedures in favor of a practical, down-to-earth list of guiding values can help you and your organization make decisions effectively and efficiently. An important question needs to be addressed when making a decision: Does this course of action fit your – or the organization's – core values, vision, and goals?

You Can Improve Your Decision-Making Skills

People are different; so are their styles of decision-making. When it comes to making a decision, one size hardly fits all. An approach that worked well in one situation may fall short under different circumstances. Below is a sequence of steps that serve as a guide for making better decisions. While simple decisions may allow skipping a step or two, complex decisions may require a step that's not listed here, such as obtaining stakeholder approval. The following is the basic framework you can use to build upon.

Decision-Making Framework:

1. Define the objective. What problem do you need to solve? Are you solving the right problem? Ask yourself, is there another way of looking at this problem?

2. Gather and analyze relevant data. Review existing data, talk to stakeholders (including people who may hold contrary opinions to your view), consult your mentors or Bamboo Circle, and look at all the available information.

3. Identify alternatives and balance them against your guiding values, brainstorm pros and cons, and do a cost and risk analysis. On a sheet of paper, write "potential costs" on one side and "potential rewards" on the other. Draw a line down the middle and brainstorm items for each side. This will help you visually identify the best decision. Do your best to identify the consequences of each alternative.

4. Consider the worst-case scenario of your preferred decision – can you live with this? What are the unintended consequences that may result?

5. Make the decision.

6. Implement.

7. Evaluate and get feedback.

8. Make any necessary adjustments.

Bamboo Rule: Indecision causes more
problems than making mistakes.

When Not to Make a Decision

Although most decisions have time constraints, you should never make a serious or important decision when you're:

- Hungry (whether physically or just wanting something too much to think clearly)

- Angry

- Lonely

- Tired

You should HALT and take care of your needs, then regroup to make the decision; you'll be glad you did.

*Bamboo Rule: Never make a major decision while sitting
at the table. Take some time to think about it.*

Steer Clear of Groupthink

Studies have shown that in general, groups make better decisions than
do individuals – except when they suffer from "groupthink." First coined
by Yale psychologist Irving Janis in 1972, groupthink occurs when there
is a high level of cohesion within a group and also pressure to go along
with the group's decision or way of thinking. There is a fear among team
members that:

- Others know more than they do, so they just go along without
  questioning the decision or evidence.

- The decision has already been made, so there is no point in actively
  participating or questioning the decision or the facts upon which it
  was made.

Groupthink is commonly thought to be the culprit behind many famous
organizational blunders, from the Enron meltdown to the Columbia space
shuttle disaster. To avoid it in your group, and manage a group decision-
making process for optimal performance, seek diverse perspectives by
keeping the following in mind:

First, encourage dissent.

- Ensure all members feel safe enough in the group to risk being
  wrong or present an unpopular opinion. Encourage this at the beginning of each meeting.

- Ask that everyone express an opinion before any "endorsements"
  from authority figures are made.

- Remember that opinions voiced loudly or passionately are not inherently more sound or more agreed-with than those voiced quietly and calmly.

- Ask questions like, "Are we seeing this right? How do we know? What if we're wrong?"

Second, truly brainstorm.

- Prime the group before the meeting; send out questions in advance so people have time to think on their own beforehand.

- When brainstorming, write all ideas out exactly as they are given. Watch the note-taker for bias against ideas or for "revising" ideas according to his or her own interpretation.

- Suspend judgment. Avoid comments like "We did that already" or "That won't work because…" Save the evaluations for after all the ideas are on the table.

Ten Potential Pitfalls in Decision Making

We've all made bad decisions. By learning from your own mistakes, as well as those other people and organizations have made, you can look for these signs of a decision pitfall and avoid them.

1. **False hopes.** Putting expectation into something outside of your control.

2. **Waiting for a miracle.** Prolonging the decision in the hope that it will "solve itself" or the "powers that be will take care of it."

3. **Following the money.** You've invested so much towards one course of action that you're not able to make a different decision now, even if it's the "right" decision.

4. **Avoidance.** Not reflecting on the real problem.

5. **Searching for confirming information.** Making a decision, then seeking supporting information. You can find data to support any decision.

6. **Being overconfident.** This leads to complacency and operating with blinders on.

7. **Being too cautious.** Never feeling like you have enough information to make the decision. You'll have to make many decisions with limited information. You can attempt to adjust if you get new or different information.

8. **Passing the decision-making responsibility on to someone else.** Sometimes, setting up a committee or letting someone else make the decision for you is displacing the responsibility. It can also create the appearance of action without actually making a decision. Be sure the decision-making responsibility does not get lost in a "Bermuda triangle" or some other vortex.

9. **Holding on to old ways.** Be careful with statements like "This is the way we've always done it."

10. **Waiting too long.** Choosing the right alternative at the wrong time is not any better than the wrong alternative at the right time, so make the decision while you still have time.

Water The Bamboo: Lessons From the Past

Reflect on a time when you made a good decision. Think of something that's going well in your life today – it's likely connected to a good decision you made. What process did you use to make this decision? Did you do something different to contribute to a successful result? What can you take from that experience?

Decision-Making Tips

- Do your decision making on paper. Make notes and keep your ideas visible so you can consider all the relevant information equally. Create a pro/con list.

- Where possible, build in time "to sleep on it" to give your inner brain an opportunity to contribute.

- Remember that few decisions are irreversible. Although there may be consequences, you can often take steps to change your decision.

- Be sure to make your decision based on *what* is right, not *who* is right.

- Recognize that you cannot know with 100% certainty that your decision is the right one – there's a certain amount of faith required.

- Give consideration to how the decision will be implemented.

- Never regret a decision! It was the right thing to do at the time. Now focus on what is right at *this* time.

- Mentally rehearse implementation of your choice and imagine what outcomes will result.

- Once you have made the decision and have taken the appropriate first step, put the "what if's" aside and *fully commit*.

SURVIVE THE STORM

nineteen

Patience, Persistence and Perseverance

"Many of life's failures are people who did not realize how close they were to success when they gave up. Our greatest weakness lies in giving up. The most certain way to success is always to try just one more time." ~Thomas Edison

Successful people simply find a way to persist, despite the same hardships of life that others blame for their demise. Take this famous person's example: When he was a boy, his mom passed away. Later, his fiancée also died. He had the equivalent of three months of school, and people ridiculed him for his appearance. His grocery business failed and he worked for more than fifteen years to pay off his debts. So, he thought he would try politics and was frequently defeated. So he gave business another go, and failed again. His name: Abraham Lincoln.

Lincoln's Life

- 1831 – failed in business
- 1832 – defeated for the legislature
- 1833 – failed in business again
- 1835 – sweetheart died
- 1838 – defeated in his bid for speaker of the state legislature
- 1843 – defeated for Congress
- 1855 – defeated for the Senate
- 1856 – defeated for Vice-President
- 1858 – defeated for the Senate
- 1860 – elected President of the United States of America
- 1862 – son died of typhoid

Do you have Lincoln-like perseverance and patience? What makes the bamboo watering metaphor so powerful is that persistence is a universal struggle. We all have good intentions, but it's hard to keep watering our bamboo day after day, especially when challenges arise or we suffer setbacks. To know success, you must commit to nurturing your bamboo for as long as necessary, through storms, pests, and drought or any adversity that presents itself.

"If all else fails, perseverance prevails." ~ Anonymous

Lessons from Lincoln

Without a doubt Lincoln embodied extraordinary perseverance. Here are three key things to learn from Lincoln's life:

1. It's not what happens to you that determines your course; it's how you respond to what happens.

2. Your bamboo, or how you grow it, may change. If one way does not work, keep looking and searching for a way to succeed.

3. Life's difficult circumstances can be a source of strength and growth in handling the challenges that you face in the future.

Reasons to Quit Are Easy

Why plant bamboo if you are not willing to water and nurture it? People quit on their careers, dreams, and relationships all the time. The excuses are endless: personal reasons, family issues, health problems, financial difficulties and other pressing obligations. Successful people have similar hardships too, but find a reason and a way to persevere. Like Lincoln, they make the necessary adjustments to have success and leave quitting to others.

> *"The price of success comes from dedication, hard work and unremitting devotion to the things you want to see happen. Nothing worthwhile comes easily." ~ Frank Lloyd Wright*

How to Develop Perseverance and Willpower:

1. **Acknowledge that not all of your work is going to be easy.** That's why it is called work. The true test of your persistence is what you do when things get tough.

2. **Learn to march forth.** Setbacks are guaranteed; long-term success is more about how you recover. We're all in recovery from something. In this very moment every one of us is recovering from either a win or a loss. For example, it could be a promotion won or a job lost, the birth of a baby or the loss of a loved one or the "win" of a new job, client, or new marriage. The idea that *everyone* is in recovery normalizes your challenges and successes. Marching forth is a forward-looking concept: it asks, after a win or loss, "Now what?"

> ### *Bamboo Rule: Whoever recovers first wins.*

3. **Complete what you start.** Develop this trait in small ways. For example, return all phone calls within 24 hours or clean your desk at the end of each day. Find examples that work for you. Create the habit of follow-through.

4. **Break down any large project into smaller pieces.** How do you eat an elephant? One bite at a time. Breaking big goals up will make the objective seem more attainable and less overwhelming, and will give you a reinforcing sense of accomplishment along the way.

> ### *Bamboo Rule: Large accomplishments are just*
> ### *a series of small wins put together.*

5. **Find support.** Spend time with people who will help you stay on task, who believe in you, and who themselves embody a spirit of persistence. People want others to succeed, and are willing to help others – even the busiest and most accomplished of them. Find yourself a coach or a mentor who will share his or her experiences with you and remind you that you too can be persistent. Find support from your Bamboo Circle.

6. **Reclaim the persistence of a child.** Have you ever noticed that young kids rarely take no for an answer? In fact, you could call them unreasonable. If you don't have kids of your own, listen to a two- or three-year-old in the candy aisle of the store. Kids are more concerned about what they want than what others think. They are persistent. Not only do they ask multiple times, but will ask a variety of ways if their first attempts are rejected. When is the last time you were that persistent? Do you find yourself stopping at the first rejection? Or talking yourself out of asking in the first place, even when it's something you really want?

7. **Expect resistance.** Resistance is a sign that you may be on the right track to growth. View resistance as an exciting challenge rather than a threat or annoyance. Some obstacles we have no control over, so stop worrying about them and get on with watering your bamboo.

> *"That which you obtain easily, you esteem*
> *too lightly."* ~ Thomas Paine

8. **Re-evaluate your efforts from time to time.** Check in periodically with your values and vision to make sure what you're pursuing still matters to you. Be sure you are focusing only on those things that are fundamental to your vision and values.

What If These People Quit?

- The Beatles – rejected by Decca Records
- Oprah Winfrey – suffered poverty and child abuse
- Thomas Edison – 10,000 attempts at the light bulb
- Michael Jordan – cut from his high school varsity basketball team
- Ray Charles – despite blindness since childhood, became a phenomenal musician and entertainer
- Herman Melville, author of *Moby Dick* – initially rejected; book became famous long after Melville's death
- Wilma Rudolph – despite being crippled by polio at age 4, became a gold-medal Olympian
- Wright Brothers – numerous failed attempts at flying
- What about people in your own life?

Water The Bamboo: What Would Lincoln Do?

Take a moment and think about people you consider to be accomplished. Ask them about the obstacles they have faced getting where they are now. You will be surprised by what you hear. Where in your life can you embrace the Lincoln-like qualities of patience, persistence and perseverance? What projects or relationships could use a bit more patience and perseverance?

Water The Bamboo: You've Done It Before!

Think of something you've accomplished in your life. Cite one or two setbacks that were difficult to overcome. At some point you may have thought about quitting; how did you persevere instead?

twenty

Change Happens

"Change is inevitable. It's direction that counts." ~ Gil Atkinson, inventor

You have either just gone through change, are going through change now, or are about to go through change. The world is in a continual state of change. With the pace of technology, even change has changed. Since change is the only constant, we must learn to embrace it. Are you prepared and flexible enough?

Like the bamboo plant itself, you must be strong *and* flexible to have success. Once you start, there will inevitably be some change in circumstance, information, or the environment. How you deal with this change will be crucial to your success. Have faith in your plan, your abilities and your approach, but don't be so rigid that a strong wind will break you. Be open to feedback and be prepared to make the adjustments necessary for success.

> ***Bamboo Example:*** *A monk goes to a hot dog stand and asks the hotdog vendor to make him one with everything. After a brief*

chuckle the hotdog vendor makes a hotdog with all the condiments, including sauerkraut. The hotdog vendor asks for $2.50 and the monk gives him a crisp five-dollar bill. After waiting a while for his change, the monk interrupts the hotdog vendor and says, "Where is my change?" The hotdog vendor replies, "Change? Change comes from within!"

As the story above alludes to, for true change to occur, it must come from inside of you. Once you make the decision to make or embrace a change, your success stems from your ability to internalize that change. Change accepted from the inside is longer lasting and more effective than something you just go along with on the surface.

Five Stages in the Change Process

In order to maintain the strength of your convictions about your bamboo – and at the same time handle change with flexibility and adaptability – it's helpful to understand the five most common stages of change. These apply to any type of change initiative that you intentionally launch, as well as to change that comes to you externally or unexpectedly. Use this model to recognize where you are now, and what to do as you progress through change. It can also help to better understand what others who are affected by change are experiencing. By understanding the five stages of change, you can create a solid change management strategy and maximize effectiveness.

1. **Commitment or acceptance.** You've just encountered change. Whether you're fully committed or just starting to accept the change at this stage, resistance is usually at its peak. At this juncture, people often report a feeling of loss or sadness, especially if it is a change they feel is imposed on them without their consent. Relax: did you forget already that the only constant is change? Re-group and stay committed to what matters. Find out as much as you can about what to expect now that things have changed. This will help you manage your expectations. Check your assumptions, too – ask lots of open-

ended questions and *listen* to the answers. You are on a fact-finding mission to see how this new change will shape your future. Stay on point and keep focused.

2. **Pain or discomfort.** This is where people often go back to the old behavior because it's more comfortable. You may feel at your worst at this stage: a combination of despair and confusion. It might feel like two steps forward and one step back for a while. Step back to get perspective. Be patient. Do things to release your stress, such as exercising. Breathe. Know that this stage will end, too. You are in control of your emotions; do not let them control your behavior or actions.

3. **Power.** You don't need as much external support and you can begin to identify with the "new" way. You're self-motivated with the change. Acknowledge yourself for having come this far. Celebrate your accomplishment, but keep in mind that you are still in the process. Maintain balance and focus.

4. **Harmony.** Harmony means "in tune with." You are fully in tune with the change. You feel as if "it has always been this way." You're ready for what's next. Rest, but be ready.

5. **What's next.** Since change is inevitable, you have to be ready for the next change so that you're not surprised when it happens. Stay in harmony and be ready to make or accept the next change…it's coming!

Proactively predict and prepare for what might come your way. The more you can understand what happens during change, the easier it is to go through it. Embrace change because it's here to stay.

People need the most support in stages one and two. Rely on your peers and your Bamboo Circle to help you through these stages. Face change knowing that you have within you the power to respond to it with grace, flexibility and strength.

Water The Bamboo: Past Successes

Understanding past success with change can help you manage future change. Think of a change that you recently made where you experienced all five stages of change. What was it like in each stage? How did you cope? Why do you think you were successful in moving through the stages?

Tips to Remember:

1. Each stage of change is temporary (although we have a tendency to remember the pain and discomfort stage the most). Know you'll get through it. You have gone through these stages before in some capacity.

2. You may slip back to an earlier stage; don't worry – that's normal.

3. Find support – mentors, colleagues, other resources, etc.

4. Build in time for rest. Recovering from change is just as important as weathering it.

5. Don't expect people to move through the stages of change at the same rate.

6. Remember what's at stake. Why is it important to weather this change well?

7. Review what you learn.

twenty-one

Busy But Balanced

"You can have it all, just not all at once." ~ *Oprah Winfrey*

We were sold the computer with two promises: we would work less and use less paper. Neither of these has happened. While technology has tripled the speed of our communications and our expectations, users more often feel overwhelmed and stressed rather than relaxed and balanced. Computers, PDAs, cell phones, the Internet and e-mail have created an intense pressure to process information and tasks almost instantaneously. In response, people are working longer and commuting in from everywhere; they're sleeping less and aren't taking breaks from their hectic schedules for fear that they will just get further behind.

Obviously, technology isn't the only reason people are struggling with balance – there are lots of other demands that pull us in many directions. As you're pursuing your bamboo, you'll have to fight against those powerful and competing forces. If you're like most people, you want success, but you also want balance and harmony in your life.

That Elusive Work-Life Balance

When you are at home, is your mind preoccupied with work? When you are at work, is your mind preoccupied with home? This may not be a result of lack of focus, but an indication that you lack balance in your life.

Though work-life balance is one of the most tossed-about buzzwords in the modern workplace, it continues to be hard for organizations to support and individuals to achieve.

What Does Balance Mean to You?

According to Webster's, balance means "to be in equilibrium." Nothing is unduly emphasized at the expense of the rest. Balance may look different to you than to your best friend. It may mean one thing to you now and something else at a different stage in your life. *Since you're the only one who can determine what balance would look like for you, it's important that you take time to clarify that picture.* The work you've done on your values, vision and goals should help with this task.

> *Bamboo Rule: As the flight attendants say, put your mask on first before helping others.*

Balance Your Life

Though it's nearly impossible to be in balance all the time – temporary shifts of priorities are inevitable – you can't sustain imbalance over the long term without damaging your quality of life. Just as you should not drive your car without getting a tune-up, changing the oil and checking the tires, you need to do the same for yourself.

What Can You Do?

Picture a three-legged stool: a leg each for time, money and energy. Keep these in balance and directed towards things that matter to you most. Use the following strategies to keep equilibrium in your life.

The 80/20 Rule. The 80/20 rule states that 80 percent of effects come from 20 percent of the causes. For example, 80 percent of your results are caused by 20 percent of your efforts. Eighty percent of your profits are from 20 percent of your clients. This is an important concept to consider as you're choosing how to spend your resources. Focus your efforts on the 20 percent that contribute to the greatest results.

Take a break. Schedule a renewing vacation, so you can give your mind, body and spirit a chance to recover. If that's not possible, take a day or two off to focus on rest and recovery. Don't over-schedule your break with a bunch of activities; the point is to give yourself a breather.

Bamboo Rule: A balanced life requires you to breathe deeply.

Develop daily practices to nourish your spirit. Build renewal into your daily schedule, so that vacations aren't the only chance you get to recharge your batteries. Use meditation, prayer, exercise, daydreaming, spending time outside, reading inspirational quotes or books, whatever it takes. Do it on a regular basis – view it as self-maintenance.

Manage your time. A lot of stress and imbalance comes from being disorganized or taking on more than you can possibly do in the time you have. Be realistic, and take time each morning to plan your day. It's also helpful to plan the week ahead as your last activity of the week. This way, you can tell ahead of time whether there's too much on your plate and begin to delegate or defer some of your workload.

Make sure you're doing the most important things first – in work and non-work – so that you can experience a sense of accomplishment and calm at the end of each day. If you can't get your most important work done in an eight- or nine-hour day, take a look at why:

- Are you addressing the most important things first, or do emails, phone calls and meetings sidetrack you? Check email on a set schedule. Let calls go to voicemail and deal with them in chunks. Allow yourself work time between meetings, as well as time to gather your thoughts and recharge.

- Avoid multitasking; instead focus on one thing at a time, to completion. Create blocks of uninterrupted work time on your calendar so that your day doesn't get swallowed up. Make yourself unavailable when working on important projects.

Create boundaries between your personal and professional life. Reign in that impulse to take work home. When you are at work, by all means work. When you're home, turn your mind to your personal life and your family.

Practice saying "no." This is one of the hardest things for most people to do, both at work and in their personal lives. Learn to say no, both to others and to all the things you tend to fill your life with. It's okay to have lots of friends and lots of commitments if you are able to nourish what's most important to you. But when things get out of balance, start looking for ways to reduce what's on your plate. You will create a better professional reputation, be more effective and satisfied, and have more fun and harmony in your personal life if you practice saying no to things that do not contribute to your bamboo.

Other Ideas to Practice:

- Unplug and do nothing

- Create a "*not* to do" list

- Get good rest regularly

- Pamper yourself every once in a while; put yourself on the calendar by taking personal time

- Learn to breathe deeply; it has an immediate, calming effect

- Pace your life a little more slowly – slow down when driving, walking, talking, eating and connecting with others

- Share the load – you don't have to be a hero or do it all yourself

Water The Bamboo: Check Your Balance

What seems out of balance in your life? What can you do or stop doing to tip the scales to achieve more balance? For one week, keep track of how you spend all of your time and energy, and compare that to what you want, referring to your values, vision and goals as needed.

Water The Bamboo: Celebrate a Value Each Week

Create a card for each of your values and rotate your focus each week. Be especially aware of doing things that support that value, but don't ignore your other core values while you're focusing on your "value of the week." For example, if one of your values is fun, you might make a special effort to inject more fun into everything you do.

now

It's Harvest Time

I t's harvest time! You've done the work: you've watered your bamboo faithfully, you've weeded, and you have survived storms. Your bamboo is sky high.

It's time to claim the rewards of your labor. There is joy and excitement in seeing the bountiful fruits of your efforts and in knowing that your work has paid off. But, there also may be more work than ever.

Now the Work Really Begins

Harvest time is a brief period compared to the years it takes to sow the seed, but it can also be the busiest time for you, so you should be ready and fully engaged. You have built your new facility, launched your new product, marketed your new service, or won that critical new client. You have to be prepared to follow through on what you've created. You'll have new demands on you. This is a period of great excitement and fulfillment, but it's also time to renew your focus. This is where you will jump to the next level – the place all your prior work was setting you up for. Your goal is to do this with your values intact.

Harvest Builds Community

A good harvest builds community and a common bond. It's a time for everyone to come together not just to rejoice, but also to bring the crops in. There is work in every direction, especially when the crop is abundant. To manage it, you may need to bring in additional help. This is a great opportunity to remind your community of why you've grown this bamboo and how you want it harvested, so that everyone approaches the harvest with clarity and enthusiasm.

Don't Let Harvest Time Pass

Reserve some energy as you watch for the signs that it's time to harvest. Timing is critical. It is ineffective to harvest before harvest time; it is likewise an error to neglect harvest work during harvest time. Don't let the opportune time to harvest pass you by. When the harvest work is complete, there will be time to rest and the growing cycle will begin anew.

Bamboo Rule: Time is of no importance during harvest…you are finished when the work is done.

The great thing about bamboo is that it is sustainable: once grown, it doesn't need to be replanted. It will grow again and again, year after year. It's the same with *your* bamboo – your vision. Once you've reached the level of success that the harvest implies, that success will keep growing year after year, when you maintain it. You *don't* have to start from scratch to see new crops come up; you just have to build on what you've created with the first crop.

"Take rest; a field that has rested gives a bountiful crop."
~ Publius Ovidius Naso "Ovid", poet

Rest and Relaxation

The value of rest after a major accomplishment can't be overstated. No matter how you do it, find a way to replenish yourself. It's tempting to just plow on to the next thing once you've completed the harvest. But don't skip the rest and relaxation. The beauty of the growing cycle is that it gives the soil – and the farmer – time to regenerate. Stop and acknowledge what you've already done. Don't assign yourself or your team the next demanding project right on the heels of the last. All too often, the only reward for doing the demanding work or completing a difficult project is another demanding and difficult project. Give yourself and your group a breather – you'll all be more prepared and motivated to tackle the next thing when it comes along.

Celebrate Your Accomplishments

In this fast-paced world, it's easy for individuals and groups to overlook the value of celebrating what they've accomplished. Teams repeatedly go the extra mile, but their celebrations are either cursory pats on the back or non-existent. Stop and really take time to recognize the achievements and efforts you and your team have made. Celebration can motivate and inspire others; it's just what is needed after one big push and before the next one. You don't have to wait until harvest time to celebrate; milestones met are a great opportunity too.

There are lots of ways to celebrate, aside from the typical group party in the meeting room. Here are a few to get you started:

- Personal notes
- Gift certificates
- Day(s) off
- Cash bonuses
- Ask team members for their ideas

No matter how you do it, look for inclusive celebrations – not everyone celebrates the same way. Having a golf outing can be unappealing to team members who don't play.

Bamboo Rule: Deliver recognition in a way that makes the recipient feel the significance of their contribution.

Include and appreciate everyone who played a role, including vendors, other departments and family members who have sacrificed. Celebrate with your Bamboo Circle, too, and acknowledge their contributions to your success. Share the wealth, the credit and the learning.

Acknowledge the Journey

- Acknowledge yourself
- Acknowledge the people who helped you
- Keep a journal of how you arrived
  - Most memorable moments
  - Most challenging times
  - What surprised you

Bamboo Rule: The journey is the destination.

Preserve the Harvest

During the harvest, capture all the expertise you gain from both your good harvests and your poor ones by taking notes about what worked, what didn't, and what you will do differently next time. That will help new team members get up to speed more quickly, and will illuminate the process of your bamboo-watering experience for those who may be in your shoes later.

Disappointing Harvests

In life, as in bamboo farming, there are no guarantees. While a harvest can be disappointing if the results don't meet your expectations, all harvests must be preserved for the lessons they teach. If your harvest is less than you desired, appreciate what success you did have, recognize those who contributed to it, and learn from the lessons provided in this experience so that you can apply them next time.

Bamboo Rule: In a banner year, save some of your bounty for years when the harvest is leaner.

Help Others with Their Bamboo

After your harvest has come in, consider giving back. Now, as you're pausing between projects, can you take some time to focus on others? Teach others how to farm bamboo of their own. You might also consider joining someone else's Bamboo Circle to help them achieve their vision. Perhaps someone from your own Bamboo Circle needs extra help. No matter how you approach it, you can make a difference in someone else's life. There's no better time to do so than once you've made a difference in your own.

Parting Thoughts

Whether you plant your bamboo seed and water it or not, the years it takes to grow your bamboo will pass. The choice of becoming a bamboo farmer is yours. It is my hope that you pursue your bamboo with unwavering faith and determination. As you continue your journey, be sure to take your core values with you – live them no matter what results you get in life. Life is a precious gift never to be taken for granted.

I am confident that a commitment to the exercises and strategies in this book – combined with your desire to achieve your vision – will leave you excited about the possibilities you can create for yourself and others.

Expect great things, and continue to water the bamboo!

When the sun rises, I go to work;
When the sun sets, I take my rest;
I dig the well from which I drink;
I farm the soil that yields my food;
I share creation – kings do no more.

~ Chinese folk poem, ca. 2000 B.C.

Index

Symbols
21 days, 63, 64, 70
80/20 Rule, 145

A
Action, 4, 12, 17, 19, 20, 28, 29, 31, 54, 59, 62, 75, 82, 85, 110, 114, 115, 116, 119, 120, 124, 127, 128
Administrative Assistants' Day, 79
Affirmations, 56, 57, 63, 69, 70, 71
Andretti, Mario, 118
Andrews, Harry, 69
Appreciation, 4, 17, 77, 78, 79, 80
Armstrong, Lance, 35
Assessment, 4, 64
Auditory, 97

B
Balanced, xii, 143
Bamboo Assessment, 4
Bamboo Circle, xi, 45, 46, 48, 49, 57, 63, 116, 124, 136, 141, 152, 153, 161
Bannister, Roger, 69
The Beatles, 138
Belief, 11, 14, 19, 53, 54, 55, 56, 57, 70
Blanchard, Ken, 45
Boundaries, 90, 146
Bristol, Claude M., 57
Buffet, Warren, 59
Build Trust, 37
Butchart Gardens, 107

C
Change, xii, 13, 139, 140, 158, 160
Change Process, 140
Charles, Ray, 138
Clarity, 3, 10, 98, 103, 150

About the Author

Greg Bell
Founder, Water The Bamboo Center For Leadership

Greg spent much of his early life on a farm in rural Texas, collecting gems of wisdom his grandfather shared with him daily. He used them well and earned bachelors and law degrees at the University of Oregon. While there, Greg competed in college basketball and was consistently named Inspirational Player of the Year.

After college, Greg worked as a lawyer for a number of years and learned how to thrive within a large organization. Upon reevaluating his life, he began looking for something that would inspire him and help others. He found it by helping launch the Coaches vs. Cancer campaign for the National Association of Basketball Coaches. This ongoing program has raised over $50 million dollars for cancer research.

Today, Greg is a recognized thought leader and founder of the Water The Bamboo Center For Leadership. As a student and keen observer of highly successful people and teams, he distilled his findings into the Water The Bamboo methodology. Through his entertaining and content-driven key-notes and seminars he has encouraged and inspired thousands of people and teams to identify and water their bamboo to remarkable results.

Participants in Greg's programs consistently say he is inspiring and thought-provoking, and that his program is the best they've attended in years. His audiences include companies, organizations and associations of all sizes and disciplines.

Greg lives in Portland, OR and is happily married with three daughters, whose middle names are Grace, Hope and Joy.

Water The Bamboo Center For Leadership

To learn more about Greg's programs and the Center's broad range of services, or to book Greg for your event, visit waterthebamboo.com or call 1-877-833-3552. Greg looks forward to customizing a program for your next event!

Recommended Reading

Blanchard, Kenneth, Ph.D. and Johnson, Spencer, M.D. *The One Minute Manager.* New York: The Berkley Publishing Group, 1983.

Buckingham, Marcus. *Now, Discover Your Strengths.* New York: The Free Press/ Simon & Schuster, Inc. 2001

Clearly, Thomas. *The Art of War: Sun Tzu.* Boston: Shambhala Publications, Inc., 1988.

Collins, Jim. *Good to Great: Why Some Companies Make the Leap...and Others Don't.* New York: HarperCollins Publishers, Inc., 2001.

Connolly, Mickey and Richard Rianoshek. *The Communication Catalyst: The Fast (But Not Stupid) Track to Value for Customers, Investors, and Employees.* Dearborn Trade Books, 2002.

Covey, Stephen. *The 7 Habits of Highly Effective People: Powerful Lessons in Personal Change.* New York: Fireside/Simon & Schuster, Inc., 1990.

Covey, Stephen M.R with Merrill, Rebecca. *The Speed of Trust: The One Thing That Changes Everything.* New York: Free Press/Simon & Schuster, 2006.

Frankl, Viktor, *Man's Search for Meaning.* Boston: Beacon Press, 2006.

Gladwell, Malcolm. *The Tipping Point: How Little Things Can Make a Big Difference.* New York: Back Bay Books/Time Warner Book Group, 2002.

Levitt, Steven D., Stephen J. Dubner, *Freakonomics; A Rogue Economist Explores the Hidden Side of Everything.* New York: William Morrow & Company, 2006.

Mapes, James. *Quantum Leap Thinking: An Owner's Guide to the Mind.* Los Angeles: Dove Books, 1996.

Scott, Susan. *Fierce Conversations: Achieving Success at Work & in Life, One Conversation at a Time.* New York: The Berkley Publishing Group, 2004.

Senge, Peter, Art Kleiner, Charlotte Roberts, Richard B. Ross, and Bryan J. Smith. *The Fifth Discipline Fieldbook.* New York: Doubleday, 1994.

Tracy, Brian. *Eat That Frog!: 21 Great Ways to Stop Procrastinating and Get More Done in Less Time.* San Francisco: Berrett-Koehler Publishers, Inc., 2007.

Don't Farm Alone – Stay Connected

Visit Our Website

For extra support and tools as you're watering the bamboo, visit <u>waterthebamboo.com</u>.

Receive Our E-Newsletter

Receive helpful reminders and tips as you're watering the bamboo. Sign up at <u>waterthebamboo.com</u>.

Form a Bamboo Circle

Form your own Bamboo Circle! Tips and ideas for creating a circle of support are available at <u>waterthebamboo.com</u> as well as in Chapter Five of *Water The Bamboo*.

Participate in the Discussion

To see what others are saying about the *Water The Bamboo* concept and to post your comments, sign up for social networks at <u>waterthebamboo.com</u>.

For more information, visit **waterthebamboo.com**.

LaVergne, TN USA
14 February 2010
173057LV00002B/1/P